Kicking Depression's Ugly Butt
Tried and True Methods for Outsmarting Depression

By

Robert Westermeyer, Ph.D.

QUICK PRINTS

Quick Publishing, LC

Printed in the United States of America

Quick Publishing, LC
1610 Long Leaf Circle
St. Louis, MO 63146

International Standard Book Number 1-882-34907-5

Contents

Foreward

By Raymond A. Fidaleo, M.D.

As director of the inpatient and outpatient cognitive therapy programs, I am proud to have been a part of a clinical restructuring that has, among other innovative changes, made Sharp Mesa Vista Hospital the most respected psychiatric hospital in San Diego. In 1985, I was given the challenge to develop a cognitive treatment program for inpatients based on Aaron T. Beck's cognitive model of therapy. Up until that time, standard hospital therapy consisted of structured activities, process group therapy, psychotropic medications and electroconvulsive therapy. There was no theoretical basis, and the goal was not to help patients learn to help themselves, but to medicate and remove people from their real world stressors. I elected to create an environment where the staff, not just the psychologist, but also the social workers, nurses, and mental health workers, and all those who had contact with the patients, would have a consistent theoretical focus and approach with them.

How did this new environment differ from previous inpatient settings? For one, patients were no longer treated simply as recipients of care; rather, they became collaborators. Cognitive therapy is a psycho-educational treatment in which hypotheses are derived via a partnership between the therapist and the patient. Patients are viewed as students, and the therapist's role is to teach these patients new ways to change and manage their moods and life stressors, and to solve their problems more efficiently. Patients are expected to practice these skills and by so doing, treat their depression.

This form of therapy was exciting to me because it was more respectful to the patient and seemed more empowering, as the patient was being taught to solve those issues that resulted in the depression and how to actually change the depressed mood itself. As the program gained respect in the community, researchers at the Department of Psychology at

San Diego State University and the University of California, San Diego, studied this population base of depressed patients. Patients left the hospital not only less depressed but equipped with tools that they could use to help themselves stay well. Medication would be part of the therapy, but not the entire therapy.

There have been many changes in mental health since those glory days. Not all changes are for the worse. Length of psychiatric inpatient stay has decreased substantially. Inpatient units are viewed as the highest level of care and are limited to those who are either incapable of caring for themselves or are at imminent risk of self-harm or harm to others. Therapy in hospitals is now delivered in outpatient treatment programs, and at Sharp Mesa Vista Hospital the form is an intensive cognitive therapy treatment program. Dr. Westermeyer was instrumental in the development of the outpatient cognitive program and was the author of much of the material that has been used in the program. He is certainly a pioneer in the development of the half-day model which is now used to replace full-day hospital inpatient treatment and even the full-day partial hospitalization model. He accepted the responsibility of working with patients who were literally in the throes of severe depression, who in the past would have been treated as inpatients for two or three weeks. Through his energy and his creative skills he was able to introduce a more focused and helpful cognitive approach for patient care that allowed the groups to accept new members on a continuous basis, another first for the outpatient treatment. This in itself was a marked departure from the way cognitive groups had been approached before.

The idea of an open cognitive group had really not been developed, as cognitive group therapy was always set up on a time-limited approach, with 12 to 18 sessions. To Dr. Westermeyer's credit, and to the benefit of the patients that he and the cognitive team worked with, the patients had not the thought that they were receiving a less substantial form of treatment but that this was the superlative treatment to the brief inpatient care they had received. They got better, they learned skills, and they were able to be at home dealing with the realities of day to day life while getting well.

I am thrilled that Dr. Westermeyer has written this book for the general public. I believe it will be of great benefit to many people.

Raymond A. Fidaleo, M.D.
Director, Cognitive Therapy Programs
Sharp Mesa Vista Hospital
San Diego, California

Preface

Searching the self-help section of your local bookstore without a specific title in mind can feel like a game of darts. Given the tremendous variety of psychological theories, it's not uncommon for the same problem to be approached from a dozen different vantage points. One book may be completely contradictory of another in its view of the problem and suggestions for recovery. Some self-help authors purport that the information they are offering will help you without any evidence to support their claims other than personal experience or good intentions. Most people who are not in the field of psychology or counseling don't keep up with the latest research as to what has the most scientific support.

As a psychologist who treats depression, I've always strived to apply the most up to date, research driven interventions. My goal in writing this book was no different. When it comes to psychology, so much of what is discovered in the ivory tower never makes it to the street, much less the self-help section.

One thing you'll notice right off the bat is that this book has a lot of references to research studies. This may strike you as different from other self-help books you've read. Most of the credit for *Kicking Depression's Ugly Butt* goes to the numerous cited researchers upon whose hard work most of the suggestions of this book are based. It is certainly not my intention to direct you to all these journal articles and academic chapters, but, in addition to respectfully giving credit to these researchers, to constantly remind you that the models and techniques presented are not driven solely by personal experience, or by inspiration, but by science.

The greatest challenge in writing this book was not in grounding each chapter in science, but doing so in a way that didn't yield a boring book. No depressed person wants to wade through a dry dissertation. *Kicking Depression's Ugly Butt* is far from boring. You will discover that esoteric language and psychological jargon have been kept at a minimum.

Some self-help books are super long, and consequently can be daunting for a depressed person. The limitations in concentration many depressed people experience too can make trudging through a four-inch-thick self-help tome seem like a calculus course. Based on my experience treating depressed patients, I believe *Kicking Depression's Ugly Butt* covers just enough: not too short, not too long.

At times, humor is also used in the presentation of concepts, exercises, and especially obstacles. There is nothing funny about depression, but if humor can distract enough to bring a smile or a chuckle, it definitely doesn't hurt. My hope is that you will find *Kicking Depression's Ugly Butt* to read like a "fun textbook."

In Chapter One you'll learn that, although the depression feels formless, there are specific symptoms, some of which are tangible, that is, modifiable. Depression is perpetuated by its symptoms. For example, depression causes negative thinking, withdrawal, and inactivity, and these symptoms, in turn, make you feel more depressed. The more depressed you feel, the more you think negatively, withdraw, and reduce activity. It's a nasty self-feeding cycle. You'll learn that gaining control over your depression requires preventing these symptoms from "invigorating" the state.

After reading Chapter Two, you will understand that depression doesn't just vanish. Recovery is patchy. Depressed people experience many changes in their mood throughout the day, even if none of these periods could be considered "happy." These brief "ups" are periods in which the depression is actually losing its strength. However, given the power of clinical depression, these patches don't last. Increasing patches of relief by modifying your thinking and behavior is the thrust of the cognitive behavioral approach.

The concept of "metacognition" (a ten-dollar word borrowed from the information processing nomenclature) is defined in Chapter Three as "thinking about thinking." This uniquely human ability, it is stressed, needs to be given workouts throughout the day. These workouts will include recognizing and stopping negative self-absorption, recognizing and disputing distorted thoughts, and redirecting your behavior.

Chapter Four introduces the first of a number of paper and pencil exercises I use in cognitive therapy. Cognitive therapy always involves some sort of step-by-step "thought record" for monitoring negative automatic thoughts and beliefs—that is, those that occur involuntarily—and testing their accuracy. The documentation of thought errors and successful disputation in black and white really helps drive home the efficacy of cognitive strategies. I have used a variety of thought record versions, and in this chapter I offer a modified flow sheet that has evolved over the years and is the version most preferred by the depressed people I've worked with.

Not all cognitive techniques are helpful to everyone. Building on the Thought Record Flow Sheet Exercise, Chapter Five offers a variety of easier and quicker methods of disallowing negative thoughts to survive. The more times you successfully alter depressive thinking, the easier and more natural it becomes.

Chapter Six focuses on the influence of depression on socialization. Depression can make us seem less inviting to others. We definitely don't want to push people away when we're depressed, but depression may cause negative changes in the areas of hygiene and attire, body language, and verbal communication. Regular monitoring and practice of positive social skills is an important part of recovering from depression.

Chapter Seven tackles anxiety, "depression's ugly little friend." Depression and anxiety often go hand in hand, and as it is with depression, identification of the "tangible" symptoms enables you to gain control of what many people report to be the most excruciating part of their depression.

Withdrawal and avoidance are classic symptoms of depression. Chapter Eight offers a model borrowed from a well-researched addictive behavior treatment strategy, and an exercise that can help you increase your motivation to get up, get moving, socialize, and do cognitive exercises; you know, all the things depression makes seem undoable, unnecessary, and uninteresting.

Kicking Depression's Ugly Butt would not be a complete K.O. without focus on anger. In Chapter Nine you will learn how anger can influence depression, especially when you don't have sufficient control over the emotion, or when it gets "stuffed down" or morphs into shame and guilt.

My first goal in writing this book was to help you extract yourself from depression. The second goal, which is equally important, is for you to become equipped with tools for keeping future episodes from occurring. The focus of Chapters Ten, Eleven and Twelve is relapse prevention. The nuts and bolts of relapse prevention are the ability to recognize early warning signs, identify and prepare for stressors in your life that could send you back into depression, and, most importantly, keeping "normal" dips in mood from becoming full blown relapses. Coming out of depression is also an opportunity to "upgrade" your lifestyle. People just coming out of a depression are often ready and willing to make changes in their lives (e.g., career, relationship, leisure time, self-improvement). Why? Because as someone rises from the gloom of depression, he or she is most motivated to not go back, to create lifestyle and interpersonal buffers that make relapse less likely. However, if that person does not venture through this "window of opportunity" when it is present, it can quickly slam shut.

Based on some exciting research from the United Kingdom, an "evolutionary" conceptualization of depression is also presented. Symptoms of depression are viewed as having served a valuable survival function when our ancestors faced defeat. In essence, when we realize we've lost, there is a hard-wired mechanism that forces us to "act defeated" (for example, by frowning, feeling bad, backing down, experiencing low energy) and thereby moving us out of the fray and preventing further harm. In most instances, the defeated party would back down, accept subordination, move away and then feel fine again. Clinical depression is viewed as the inability to get out of a defeat state. The chapter stresses the importance of identifying aspects of your lifestyle or thinking that keep you in a defeated state, as well as ways to regain power and/or move away from the sources of defeat.

The last chapter presents some of my views on medication and therapy. A self-help book that really rings true theoretically and offers some new information can be very helpful as you work your way out of depression. Information can drive change all by itself. I've seen it happen to others; it's happened to me. When people suffer depression, the sooner it is broken the better. As depressions endure, they become harder to break. It's stressed repeatedly throughout the book that it's important to hit depression from all fronts. See your doctor and discuss whether antidepressant medication is appropriate. There have been remarkable improvements in medications used to treat depression in the past two decades. In addition, individual or group therapy can help you gain insight about your depression and its causes, and teach you better ways of coping.

Acknowledgements

I want to thank Angie Quick, publisher, for her enthusiasm and her contributions to the design and text itself; Tracey Johnson, editor, for her simplifications of the sometimes esoteric verbiage of a psychologist; Karen Fiorino, illustrator, for her meticulous attention to the illustrations and cover design; and Joel Leach, for his faith in this book. Raymond Fidaleo, M.D., helped hone early versions of the book. His extensive knowledge of cognitive therapy and wisdom with regard to cognitive case conceptualization has been invaluable. Tom Horvath, Ph.D., serves as a model for the importance of remaining true to empirical research. Paul Gilbert, Ph.D., generously provided editorial help on the sections dealing with his pioneering research on the involuntary defeat strategy.

I will continue to be indebted to the Association for Advancement of Behavior Therapy (AABT) for sparking my interest in cognitive behavior therapy as a graduate student and for keeping me up to date with its conferences and journals. I want to thank Marshall Williams for lending his photographic expertise as well as encouragement with regard to this book. I also want to thank David Alford, Maria Montgomery, Debbie Brown, Dominique Ryba, and my brothers, Billy and Geoff, for their continued interest and support. And of course, special thanks goes to my wife, Monica, and my three children, Michael, Timothy, and Madeline, for providing inspiration on a regular basis.

Chapter One:

Depression: A Self-Feeding Spiral

A depressed young man named Richard once expressed to a group of fifteen or so other depressed adults what the experience was like for him. With Richard's permission, I share with you his words:

"Depression sucks. It's an awful state that exceeds tenfold any physical ache or injury I've endured. It's like this huge and filthy ogre busts into your house, plants itself on your chest, and won't get off, no matter how much you struggle. You can't move.

The depressive ogre's primary goal is to find a comfortable place to sit.

You can hardly breathe. And he's got your limbs shackled to the mattress. The thing's voracious, feasting on everything, every morsel of pleasure in the place, your tools of trade, your hobbies, and your wardrobe. Any friend or loved one who steps close enough to its snapping mouth gets bitten hard, and off they flee. Other acquaintances hear about the uninvited beast, and they just keep away. After a few weeks of this, the interior of your place looks like a prison cell, all dark and with only just a lone flickering bulb. After a while, you get so accustomed to the ogre's presence that you begin to believe that you deserve the uninvited guest; that you're somehow transforming into the most appalling and undesirable creature on earth; that your power over every aspect of your life has been snuffed out; and the only future likely is one of submitting to that awful ogre's consumption of you and your once satisfying life."

I began this chapter with Richard's description of depression because many depressed people have told me that the standard clinical descriptions of depression fall short in terms of capturing the true misery of the state. None of the other depressed patients in the group had any doubt that Richard knew depression quite well. One patient, responding to Richard, likened hers to a tar pit. Another described hers as a dark, bottomless well.

Yes, depression sucks. No two ways about it.

More than the Blues

It is very difficult for people who have not experienced depression to understand what it's like. Some people, when they hear of depression, think that it is simply a heavy bout of sadness, or an extended case of "the blues." Depression may start out like a case of the blues (a low, mildly sad, unmotivated state), but insidiously, it becomes overwhelming and feels uncontrollable. The blues and an episode of depression are far from akin. A normal case of the blues doesn't interfere significantly with one's life. Depression, on the other hand, does. For some people, it is debilitating.

Depression is also different from brief, temporary bouts of sadness in that there are many more symptoms. No case of the blues sends mood completely to the well bottom and siphons energy, motivation, and pleasure to the extent that one literally can't attend to a normal day. The blues doesn't do to thinking what depression succeeds in doing; that is,

**Though they have certain things in common, depression
and "the blues" are very different animals.**

tossing all perceived attributes and sense of power and hope
into the toilet.

Furthermore, depression doesn't tend to respond to small
perks and minor changes in the environment. A box of
chocolates may seem a reasonable perk-up for a spell of the
blues, but to a person in the throes of a clinical depression
it's about as helpful as a box of dirt clods.

Some depressed people will go on a vacation to get away
from their stressors; that is, the things that cause them stress.
Often, the vacation ends up being miserable, and upon
returning, they find the depression is no better. What people
who haven't had depression often fail to understand is that
the grisly condition is all consuming. It influences critically
important areas of functioning and isn't something from
which a person can just bounce back, especially on demand.

The good news is that these days some very effective
treatments for depression are available. The past decade
has seen the emergence of many potent new antidepressant medications, many with fewer side effects than the
frontline antidepressants of bygone days. Plus, research

**Perky tidbits of glee don't tend to
help when a person is depressed.**

has ferreted out the more effective psychotherapeutic
treatments from the large pool of available therapies. Cog-
nitive-behavior therapy, the therapy model upon which
this book is based, is one of these therapies. A great deal of
research supports cognitive behavior therapy for not only
reducing depression, but also for decreasing vulnerability
to relapse (e.g., Hollon, DeRubeis, Evans, Wiemer, Garvey,
Grove, & Tuason, 1992; Blackburn & Moore, 1997). A well-
targeted antidepressant medication plus cognitive therapy
is considered by many clinicians to be the standard treatment for depression.

Depression, Drawn In Fifths

Delineating the specific symptom components of depression will enable you to hone in on the ones that are tangible;
that is, the ones that can be changed. Why focus on the

symptoms as opposed to the causes of depression? We'll consider triggers and vulnerability when we get to relapse prevention; however, getting out of depression requires changes in your here-and-now behavior and thinking. In the words of Dr. Aaron Beck, who pioneered cognitive therapy of depression in the 1960s and '70s (Beck, 1963; Beck, Shaw, Rush, & Emery, 1979), "Each of the components has a reciprocal relationship with the other components, and, therefore, improvement in one major problem area generally spreads into the others," (Beck, et al., p.167). The five symptom categories of depression are *emotional, motivational, physical, cognitive,* and *behavioral.*

Emotional Symptoms

Most depressed people are primarily aware of changes in their mood. In fact, depression is categorized as a mood disturbance. Sadness is how most people describe it. There are nuances to this sadness that vary from person to person. Loneliness is common. The searing loneliness of depression is like you've been flung all by yourself into an empty dumpster. Guilt and shame typically rear their ugly heads, all draped in black, wielding boxes of thumbscrews and lists of bad deeds done. A depressed person's range of emotional experience tends to decrease too. It's like depression switches the full-color emotional picture tube to black and white. For some people, this experience feels like a numbing or "flattening" of mood; for others, in particular people who have an "anxious depression," it feels as if they are confined to a narrow band of unpleasant emotions.

Depressed people usually endure a host of other completely different negative emotions. It's like depression has a polarity for all the other ugly emotions we can experience. Most common are anxiety and anger, especially anxiety. The reason we want to get a handle on these other negative emotions too is that they can not only make the depressive experience more subjectively painful, but can feed it as well.

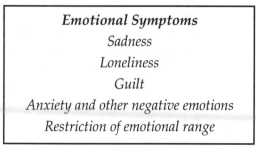

Motivational Symptoms

It's hard to get jazzed about anything due to the motivational deficits of depression: apathy, disinterest and anhedonia. Everything feels like it weighs 200 pounds. Anhedonia, which means "without pleasure," is one of the first symptoms to emerge when people are becoming depressed. It's like all the color has drained from things previously enjoyable. Interests, hobbies, and passions not only seem impossible to take part in, but not worth it. It's a vast gray landscape in which there is plenty to do, but the activities themselves have no magnetism. They're just time-fillers.

Motivational Symptoms
Anhedonia
Disinterest
Apathy

Physical Symptoms

Depression takes its toll on the body. Most depressed people report low energy and fatigue. It feels like someone came in and swiped all their bones. Other depressed people don't get lethargic so much as restless, agitated or "bottled up." One depressed woman said she felt like she'd been infused with some nasty carbonated beverage and shaken up. In fact, a psychiatrist's medication choices will be partially based on whether the depressed person is more "vegetative" or "agitated." Of course, many variables are considered when a physician makes a medication choice, but the decision to use a more sedating antidepressant or a more energizing one will often be based on whether the person needs to be helped to relax or given a bit more energy. To help the doctor choose the medication which will most likely be a good match for you, he will consider the specific symptoms of your depression, your personality, any existing medical problems, and how any possible side effects might affect you. If you are considering antidepressant medication, you might consider visiting a psychiatric specialist as opposed to a family doctor, since a psychiatrist, by definition, has more training and experience in choosing the best psychotropic medication.

Depression usually affects appetite. Most depressed people will become less hungry, and some will lose weight. But this isn't always the case. Some depressed people will put on weight when they're depressed. I recall one depressed patient claiming that an early warning sign of his depression was an increase in nightly purchases of ice cream pints. Food can be soothing, and when you're steeped in something as painful as depression, you'll do just about anything that works in terms of getting some relief. This is one reason substance abuse and depression are so intimately linked.

Diminished interest in sex is a classic symptom of depression. As it can do with hunger, depression can send libido flying south to a balmier climate. This symptom can strain relationships, especially if the intimate partner doesn't know his or her partner is depressed, or doesn't have a good understanding of the typical symptoms of depression. Keep in mind, some of the antidepressants can also affect sexual functioning. If you're taking an antidepressant and you are bothered by sexual side effects (or if any side effects seem to be defeating the purpose), talk about it with your doctor. Don't be embarrassed; such complaints are more common than you might think. And your doctor definitely doesn't want you to take it upon yourself to modify dosage or just stop taking your medication without his or her knowledge. I've found most doctors want to have a collaborative relationship with their patients.

Disturbance in sleep is very common too. Typically, individuals will either have a hard time getting to sleep or have a hard time staying asleep. In addition to insomnia, hypersomnia, or sleeping too much, is common. People will sleep 12 or more hours a day and still not feel rested. Some people will have both insomnia and hypersomnia, and then adopt the lifestyle of a night monkey, slumbering in some damp hollow log by day, then slithering inside and around the log alone by night.

Depressed people will very often have a host of bodily complaints. You name it: aches, pains, tension, nausea, cramps, and canker sores. Now, there are a couple of hypotheses as to why depressed people complain so much about how their bodies feel. One, they're so negatively focused that they're noticing things that were there all along but didn't bother them because they were either too busy or their positive moods muffled the pain; or two, the lifestyle of a depressed person invites physical problems. I think both are true. As we'll see, depression creates a self-focus that highlights the negative, and a lifestyle involving an all-day couch-bed existence, poor hygiene, and/or an unbalanced diet is a set up for cramps, tension, infections, and other bodily unease.

Physical Symptoms

Low energy
Fatigue
Agitation
Decreased sex drive
Sleep problems
Appetite disturbance

Cognitive Symptoms

"Cognitive" refers to thinking. Cognitive symptoms of depression can be divided into two categories. The first category is *impairment*, which is a change in our ability to think. The second category is *bias*, which is a change in the quality of our thinking.

Thought Impairment—Changes in Our Ability to Think

Depression makes it hard to think; hard to focus; hard to concentrate; hard to remember things that happened yesterday—and even things that happened yester-minute. Depression consumes a great deal of what is called "cognitive capacity." Cognitive capacity is the limited "space" in our information processing system for conscious, effortful thinking. Strong negative emotions tend to monopolize the limited space, leaving very little room for mental tasks such as problem solving, abstract thinking, and calculation. This is why it is often reasonable for some people to take time off work when they're very depressed. These deficits in thinking can be quite overwhelming, and if your job requires you to do a lot of concentrating, decision-making, and thinking on your feet, it's often very reasonable to take a leave and get the depression treated.

Thought Bias—Changes in the Quality of Our Thinking

Recent research has shed light on how our brains process information, and how states like depression influence how we think. Not only is it harder to think when we're depressed, but the quality of our thinking changes too. Depression distorts how we think, what we think about, and the conclusions (thoughts) that we draw from our thinking.

Bias in Thought Processes—Changes in How We Think

In researching depression, Doctors Rick Ingram and Phillip Kendall (1986) have differentiated between the action of thinking and the content of our thoughts, or our conclusions. (The authors refer to the action of thinking as a cognitive process, and to the content of our thoughts as a cognitive product.) A thought process, or thinking, is an action, like trying to remember the time of an appointment. The content of a thought is the resulting conclusion made, like "Oh, yes, I remember my appointment is at 3 P.M."

One thought (cognitive) process which depression influences is our *attention* (Ingram, 1984), which can be defined as our focus, the aiming of our senses. Think of attention like a powerful flashlight. When we're not depressed, the flashlight shines in all directions, picking up nice things, neutral things, and ugly things. When we're depressed, it's like the flashlight becomes a honing device for all that is bad, ugly, soiled, ruined, miserable, dilapidated, dark, and dismal. Most depressed people can relate to this operation by reflecting on their days and listing what they encountered. Usually the list will be heavy with negative things. Let's say

**The Depressive Ogre likes to
straddle the attentional spotlight.**

a depressed person accompanies a non-depressed person to the beach. The non-depressed person is mesmerized by the vast and splendid firmament, the wheeling gulls, the sparkling ocean surface, the indigo waves curling toward shore, and the lovely cloud formations (they look like angels). The depressed person, on the other hand, is paying little attention to all that; rather, he's distracted by the rotting seaweed piled in massive clumps, the swarm of flies hovering over the teeming trash cans and the homeless person digging in them, the cigarette butts, the dog excrement, and of course, the cloud formations (they look like demons). When we're depressed, our brains sort of get locked into negative thinking grooves, which results in negative thoughts or conclusions about ourselves and the world around us.

This spotlight on the negative is one symptom that strengthens depression. Here's how: If you're filtering out the positive and focusing on the negative all day, come sundown, how can we summarize your day? That's right; devoid of anything nice, even though it might not have been that negative at all. And since you've paid too much attention to the negative, this is the stuff you'll be mulling over and over. For example, if I were depressed and noticed a nursing home across the street, I might start thinking about Grandma's demise last year, and from that start reviewing all the losses in my life.

Another thought process symptom of depression is "negative self-focused attention." When we aren't depressed, there's a nice balance between outward-focused attention and self-focused attention. People who are not depressed can focus outwardly on their duties at work and at home, but they also have a healthy amount of self-focus where they can get absorbed in personal planning, thoughts, fantasies and what not. However, depression makes it hard to for people to get outside themselves. People who are depressed spend hours in their own skulls, and it's not fantasizing that's going on in there, either. Rather, it's a grim self-absorption; it's doubt, regret, self-punitive rumination; a recital of depression's awful symptoms.

Negative self-focused attention makes it hard to derive pleasure from things, because it keeps people from getting immersed in activities. A depressed person can leave a beautiful sunset and report that she had a miserable time. When asked about the sunset itself, she might not remember much, because while she was standing there at sundown, the sky might as well have been completely overcast given that her mind was busy recycling ugly thoughts. Negative self-absorption also makes it difficult to spend time with a depressed person, because they tend to talk too much about themselves, their problems, and how bad they feel.

Depression also influences the process of memory retrieval (e.g., Rhodes, Riskind, & Lane, 1987; D.A. Clark & Teasdale, 1985; D.M. Clark & Teasdale, 1982). Depression makes us more likely to recall the lousy events from our past than the nice or neutral ones. Even though depressed people might have just as many good memories stored as non-depressed folks, the negative memories are the ones that will bubble to the surface in the wee hours or be "activated" by neutral stimuli in the environment. Like negative attention bias, this symptom can strengthen depression too. The more we recite past negative events, the more we miss out on distractions that might pull us out of the depression for a bit. Using electric current as a metaphor, constant "turning on" of negative information processing pathways adds voltage to them, making it harder and harder to turn them off.

Bias in Thought Content—Changes in What We Think About
The circuitry of our brains processes information, both from memory and the outside environment, resulting in our conscious thoughts—our conclusions, assumptions, and attributions. Inasmuch as our thinking becomes morbidly self-focused and drawn to the negative things in life when

we're depressed, the quality of our actual thoughts changes too. It's as if reality, which used to seem okay, has morphed into something dark and miserable.

Dr. Aaron Beck and his colleagues identified three specific thought areas influenced by depression: the *self*, the *environment*, and the *future* (Beck, et al., 1979). The depressed person develops a mindset of *hopelessness*, *helplessness*, and *worthlessness*. Beck called this the "cognitive triad."

Hopelessness is the most serious of the cognitive product biases. Even when people's lives haven't worsened much, depression makes it seem as if they have. If this goes on for a while, it can seem like things are never going to get better. Depressed people don't always see their futures as hopeless, but when they do, it can be dangerous. Hopelessness tends to precede suicidal thinking. This isn't always the case. Some people have strict values forbidding suicide, and some are able to keep hopelessness in check to the extent that they don't entertain the idea of dying. However, when people do have suicidal thoughts, hopelessness is always a driving force. Interestingly, when depression lifts, even if the depressed person's situation hasn't changed a whole lot, it becomes easier to consider a hopeful future, and thoughts of suicide fly away like a defeated vulture.

If you have suicidal thoughts, you must tell someone. Not all depressed people have suicidal thoughts, but they can crop up when you're depressed, and they also tend to go away when depression lifts regardless of your situation! The Appendix offers additional information on suicide prevention.

When we're depressed, we believe that we are helpless and that our lives are uncontrollable. It seems like everything is bigger and more foreboding and dangerous. It's like someone hacked our threshold for feeling secure in half. Everything seems like an impossible disaster. Managing little Joey who doesn't want to do his homework tonight was no big deal before the depression. Now it feels completely impossible. This mindset of helplessness is one reason anxiety and depression very often go hand in hand.

Cognitive Symptoms

Thought Impairment
Confusion
Problems paying attention
Difficulty concentrating
Blocking
Difficulty problem-solving

Thought Bias	
Bias in Thought Process	*Bias in Thought Content*
Too much attention to the	*Hopelessness*
negative	*Helplessness*
Negative self-focused attention	*Worthlessness*
Dwelling on negative memories	
Mind wandering from one	
negative topic to another	

Depression often creates a sense of low self-worth. It's like our human stock value has plummeted and every day is a bear market in terms of regaining our value. Even people who felt pretty good about themselves start to come to ugly conclusions about themselves, even downright self-debasing conclusions. Thoughts like, "I'm stupid," "I'm ugly," or "I'm a failure," seem to crop up automatically in response to things that, for some people, used to be easy to brush off.

Behavioral Symptoms

Inactivity is the primary behavioral symptom of depression. People tend to do a whole lot of nothing when they're steeped in depression. And this isn't about laziness. Consider how bad depression feels all over; you'd be hard pressed to find someone who is able to keep up the same lifestyle he had before the depression hit. When someone is depressed, things don't get done. Everything feels impossibly huge, therefore nothing gets started, and the four walls of the bedroom keep the depressed person from having to face the endless piles of tasks outside. When folks are really depressed, they tend to stay in bed, or on the couch-turned-bed. This isn't always the case. Some people muster the energy to keep moving despite feeling terrible, but most notice that even routine everyday activities require a great deal of effort.

Now, you'd think that a depressed person would take advantage of opportunities to have even a tiny pleasurable respite: rent a comedy, go out and buy a fish taco, put on a favorite CD; but no. Pleasurable activities get flushed with the waste. They just don't seem like they're going to be pleasurable. When a person is depressed, everything feels like it is going to be rotten, or drudgery, or intolerably boring.

Social activity comes to a screeching halt too. Someone might have been a social butterfly before the depression, but the depression fills in all the doorways with plaster, cuts the phone wires, and disconnects the internet. Again, you'd think that the distraction of others and the medicinal words of loved ones would be desired, but that's not what happens. The company of others feels like work. Plus, depressed people don't feel like they would be good company.

In addition to a decrease in socialization, social skills go downhill. What are social skills? They are the behaviors people must have in order to interact successfully with others. In my clinical experience, I've noticed three social skill areas that are typically influenced by depression: *hygiene and attire, body language,* and *verbal communication.* When depressed, people often give less attention to their appearance, they send unattractive nonverbal signals, and their verbal communication tends to be overly negative and self-focused. Chapter Six focuses exclusively on social skill enhancement as a powerful way to help reduce depression.

> *Behavioral Symptoms*
> *Inactivity*
> *Withdrawal*
> *Reduction of pleasurable activities*
> *Decreased socialization*
> *Social skill deficits*

A Self-Feeding Spiral

All maladies have symptoms. The nasty seven-week cold I suffered one November had symptoms, including head congestion, malaise, and fever. But my cold symptoms were just symptoms. They didn't worsen or prolong the disease itself; they were just . . . symptoms. Depression is different from a cold, or the flu, or a hangover; the symptoms of depression perpetuate the state. Unchecked, the symptoms feed each other and can keep depression going for weeks, months, or years.

As you read this example, follow the illustration below.

Let's say Paula gets laid off from her job due to downsizing (event) and in response comes to conclusions like "I'm a loser; I'm unemployable." This conclusion will certainly make Paula feel sad and guilty (emotional), which in turn will lead to a lethargic, listless state (physical), to which she might elect to spend all day in bed (behavioral), leading to insomnia that evening (physical). There, with the insomnia, Paula has darkness and silence and hours to think other thoughts like "I can't do anything with my life" (cognitive) and to conjure ugly memories of past failures (cognitive). The next morning, she'll have no appetite (physical), and skip breakfast. Later in the day, she feels like her energy has been sapped (physical) and finds it hard to concentrate (cognitive). She feels unmotivated and apathetic (motiva-

Self-feeding model of depression: Paula's responses.

tional) and consequently cancels her lunch date with her friend Greg (behavioral). The mail arrives and she notices it's hard to concentrate, the gas bill is confusing (cognitive). She thinks to herself, "I can't think," and "my whole life is falling apart" (cognitive). This adds frustration and anxiety to her experience (emotional) and restlessness to her fatigue (physical), which will lead to the decision to cancel a scheduled job interview (behavioral), and so on. Each of the decisions made because of the depression then strengthens the depression, which causes the person to make even more decisions based on depression, which further strengthens the depression . . . and the cycle continues. *Depression is a pathological state that perpetuates itself by virtue of symptoms feeding symptoms.*

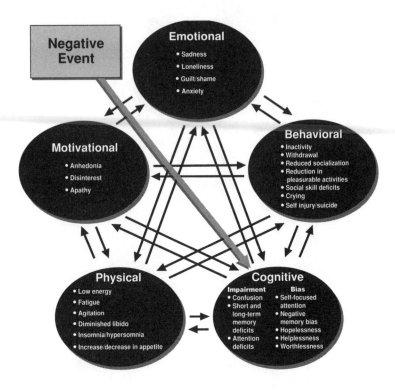

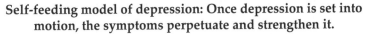

Self-feeding model of depression: Once depression is set into motion, the symptoms perpetuate and strengthen it.

Stuck in the Whirlpool

You might be thinking that getting laid off wouldn't be enough to get you depressed, or perhaps your depression has a biochemical component. Indeed, the triggers for depression vary from person to person. There are three prime causes of depression: negative events, biology, and dysfunctional beliefs.

Most depressions are caused by negative life events. Often the event is a loss, a defeat, or finding yourself powerless or trapped. It isn't just catastrophic events that can cause depression, either. What causes depression in one person could have a mild effect on another. Furthermore, small and medium sized stressors can come at you all at once, or one at a time like a string of ugly beads.

For some people, depression has a biological cause. A good example is bipolar illness, in which swings from extreme highs and extreme lows and back to depression are the product of chemical imbalance. Drugs like lithium carbonate and sodium valproate stabilize mood so it doesn't swing so much either way. Another example of biology contributing to depression is postpartum depression, in which hormonal changes caused by pregnancy and childbirth initiate depression (most researchers believe postpartum depression is a combination of biological and environmental factors). Other chemicals introduced into the body can create depression too. Coming down from cocaine or crystal methamphetamine can trigger an episode of depression.

The third cause of depression is the presence of dysfunctional beliefs. If someone believes that he is a failure, and gets turned down for a job, he'll probably assume it's because he's a failure, and he would be more vulnerable to getting depressed than someone who doesn't believe he is a failure and who might conclude after not getting a job that it was due to the competitive field, not some awful personal deficit.

One or more of these triggers can set depression into motion. Zap! Now depression sets in, and with depression come the symptoms: the negative thinking, the isolation, the reduction of pleasurable activities, the inactivity, and so on. *The more the depression creates symptoms, the more the symptoms worsen depression.*

Let's consider some of these symptoms in turn. Depression causes negative thinking, so the depressed person starts focusing on only the grim stuff in her day, entertaining only negative memories and coming to hopeless, helpless, and worthless conclusions. The more she does this, the more depressed she gets. The fewer pleasurable activities she engages in, the less frequent will be periods of even minimal respite, and consequently, her life will feel more and

Self-Feeding Depressive Spiral

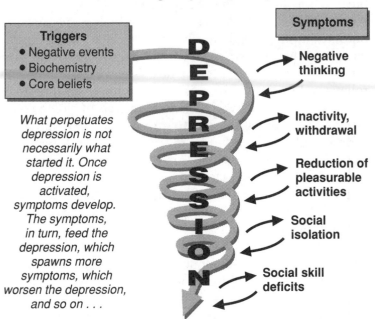

A self-feeding spiral.

more meaningless. The less she tends to responsibilities, the more helpless she feels. The less she socializes, the less she benefits from the support, the reassurance, and the "therapy" of others' words. The more her social skills are diminished, the more she pushes others away, and consequently, the more alone she feels. Depression is triggered, but the longer it endures, the less it is about the trigger and the more it is about the symptoms. *The triggers don't perpetuate depression. The symptoms do.*

Driving this principle home a third way, imagine Richard's analogy at the start of this chapter. The depressive trigger is Richard's ogre sitting at the top of a snowy hill. It shoves a snowball of depression over the hill, and as the snowball rolls downward, it gathers layers of symptoms, which get squished right onto the surface, enlarging the thing. Pretty soon, this snowball of depression is barreling breakneck over the rolling hills by its own momentum. After a while, the ogre can hardly be seen anymore. The ogre caused the whole disaster, but he isn't contributing to its continued momentum. The snowball is so big that by virtue of its accumulated layers of symptoms, it just keeps rolling on its own.

The snowball of depression rolls downhill, getting larger and larger as it adds layers of symptoms.

Good News?

The idea that depression is a self-perpetuating state is always the first concept I try to help depressed patients understand. I've found that some are often discouraged at this point. They might say something to the effect of: "Oh, great. I'm in a self-perpetuating downward spiral. Any more good news, Doc?"

Letting depression wheel on its own can result in a prolonged bout. However, consider the alternative. Imagine if there was some way to slow down the cycle; reverse it, even. Depression has symptoms, but do they necessarily *have* to feed the state? The answer is no. In the next chapter you will discover that when symptoms are stopped, the depression loses its strength. It doesn't lift right away, but slowly and begrudgingly. A person with depression has many opportunities every day to weaken that depression, but it takes focused attention and diligence to keep depression from reviving itself.

Main Points

1. Depression is distinguished from "the blues" in that it is a severe, prolonged, debilitating state from which sufferers can't just bounce back.

2. Though depression feels amorphous, it is a syndrome with identifiable symptoms. The symptom categories of depression are emotional, motivational, physical, cognitive, and behavioral. The purpose of listing the symptoms of depression is so that you can tackle the ones that you can change.

3. Though depression has many possible triggers or causes, including biochemical abnormalities, once depression is triggered, it is the symptoms that perpetuate the state.

Chapter Two:

Finding Patches of Relief

Consider the graph below. On the vertical axis is plotted mood, with negative at the bottom and positive at the top. On the horizontal axis is plotted time, starting with the morning and moving right to bedtime. See the gray line at the bottom? This is how Louis, a very depressed man who'd recently lost his job, rated his mood at bedtime for the entire day. One miserable, daylong flatliner.

This, however, is not what actually happened. This bedtime assessment was the product of a very depressed person's negatively biased memory. Depressed people are notoriously poor historians when it comes to assessing the quality of experience several hours later. Nick might ask, "How was your day, Louis?" and get this in reply: "Terrible, Nick, from sunrise to sunset."

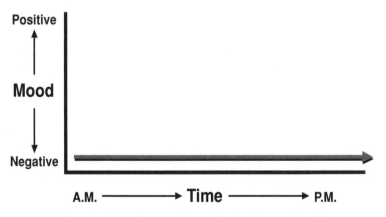

Flatliner rating of mood (gray line) taken at bedtime.

As an assignment for the following day, Louis was asked to document what he was doing every couple of hours and rate his mood. As you can see below, his hour by hour rating of mood yielded a quite different picture.

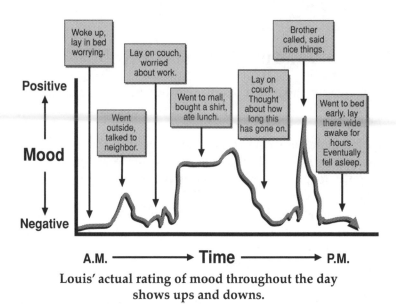

Woke up, lay in bed worrying.

Lay on couch, worried about work.

Brother called, said nice things.

Positive

Went outside, talked to neighbor.

Went to mall, bought a shirt, ate lunch.

Lay on couch. Thought about how long this has gone on.

Went to bed early, lay there wide awake for hours. Eventually fell asleep.

Mood

Negative

A.M. ─────→ Time ─────→ P.M.

Louis' actual rating of mood throughout the day shows ups and downs.

Note the spikes, the waves, and the plateaus on this graph. These are periods during which Louis felt better. Note the dips, the troughs, and the gullies. These are periods when his depression was worse.

Louis was asked what he thought about the fact that there were periods during which his depression wasn't as strong. He said, "Well, I wasn't really feeling better. The depression was still there; I was just distracted from it."

Untrue. *Though there were no periods in which Louis felt "great," these brief patches of improved mood are actually periods of lessened depression.* When depressed people rate their mood, or "self-monitor," throughout the day, they always find that there are some reliable trends to their mood changes. When the cognitive and behavioral symptoms of depression are disallowed by the environment, mood improves. Louis' intervals of improved mood were associated with such things as socialization, potentially pleasurable activities, getting things accomplished, and a hopeful attitude. Periods of low mood were associated with withdrawal, inactivity, undesirable activities and a rotten attitude.

Let's Not Wait for Spontaneous Remission

In my experience, when people's depressions lift on their own, or spontaneously remit, they do so in a patchy manner, starting with few and far between periods of relief, then more of them. Then the periods of relief fuse into extended respites; the dips get less and less extreme, and eventually the depression is gone.

Louis' graph suggests that patches of improved mood happen by accident throughout the day. Doesn't it seem reasonable that if you could somehow increase the number of patches, prolong them, and minimize dips, that recovery from depression could be hastened?

In a nutshell, this is what *Kicking Depression's Ugly Butt* is all about: using new cognitive and behavioral skills to increase patches of relief. The more patches, the weaker the depression becomes and the easier it becomes, in turn, to prolong the patches.

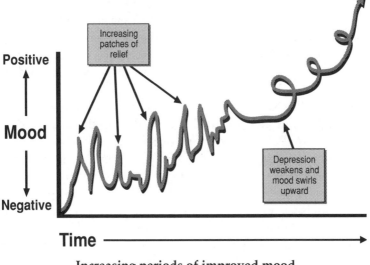

The Upward Spiral

Positive

Increasing patches of relief

Mood

Negative

Depression weakens and mood swirls upward

Time

**Increasing periods of improved mood
hasten a positive trend in mood.**

Depression Gets Its First Fist Blow

Following is a form that depicts the hours of a day. Photocopy several dozen of these, or transcribe the column labels into your organizer or calendar. The purpose of this assignment is to test the hypothesis that even though you're depressed, your mood changes a lot, and also for you to determine whether you can increase periods of relief by changing behavior and attitude.

Activity Monitoring and Planning Form

How to use the form:
1. Each day, fill out the first two columns of the Activity Monitoring and Planning form for the following day. Every hour should have some planned activity even if it's something mundane, such as showering or dressing. Attempt to plan as normal a day as possible; that is, plan to rise and retire at reasonable hours, eat regular meals, and avoid long naps. Get out of the house for several hours each day.
2. For each day, schedule at least one activity that is potentially pleasurable, at least one activity involving other people, and something that would qualify as an accomplishment.
3. In the second column, predict the degree of pleasure you anticipate deriving from the activity on a scale of zero to 10. Zero would be completely devoid of pleasure, and 10 would be bliss.
4. Keep this schedule with you throughout your day, and every hour jot down what you ended up doing as well as the actual pleasure score associated with the hour.
5. The final column is for you to begin monitoring the thoughts you're having during the day. For example, if I went to the beach by myself, and rated my pleasure at two, I might identify some thoughts like, "My life is as repetitive and meaningless as that bird running back and forth." Don't forget the thoughts column. You're going to soon find that the thoughts you have during your day are contributing more to your depression than you can imagine. Successfully altering them will prove to be your most powerful remedy.

Activity Planning and Monitoring Form

	Planned Activity	Anticipated Pleasure	Actual Activity	Actual Pleasure	Thoughts
7					
8					
9					
10					
11					
12					
1					
2					
3					
4					
5					
6					
7					
8					
9					
10					

Activity planning and monitoring may seem like impossible tasks because you feel so crummy. However, most depressed people I've worked with who followed through with the assignment reported that it wasn't nearly as difficult as they'd predicted. Also, they found that the increased structure made them feel more in control and consequently less depressed. Nonetheless, some had a hard time getting started. Below are some common attitudinal obstacles you may encounter, as well as some ways to keep the beliefs from blocking your progress.

Planning and Engaging In Pleasurable Activities

First problem: "Nothing brings me pleasure."

Response: As previously discussed, that's fairly common with depression. If you allow anhedonia to keep you holed up in your apartment or bedroom, you're probably going to stay depressed longer. If, on the other hand, you put the cart before the horse (engaging in a potentially pleasurable activity before the actual experience of pleasure or motivation to do so) you may find that reprieves from depression are possible.

Second problem: "I don't have money to take a vacation."

Response: Pleasurable activities don't need to be grand; in fact, small frequent ones that link the boring in-between hours are the goal. Taking a relaxing bath, going window shopping, going out for your favorite food even if it's out of the way, buying a new shade of lipstick, renting *Animal House* because you laughed thunderously when you saw it in college are the sorts of things that seemed to plant themselves in your day all by themselves before you were depressed. Try to assign something potentially pleasurable during predictably difficult times of the day. Morning is the worst time for many depressed people. For others, sundown is a hard time. Something like walking the dog at sunset may not have the power to turn the waning day into ecstasy, but it might be enough to distract you enough that you don't dread the dusk of tomorrow, and you might even look forward to it.

A good way of finding appropriate assignments is to take a sheet of paper and go strolling down Memory Lane, compiling an exhaustive pleasurable activities inventory. List all the stuff you used to do, big and small, that brought some pleasure to your day. Then start planting these previously pleasurable activities into your days and see what happens.

Planning and Following through with Accomplishment Tasks

Problem: "Everything feels impossible. The house is a complete mess, and the bills are all unpaid and strewn amid the mess. I can't go back to work yet."

Response: Depression siphons energy, drive, and ambition. Of course things are hard to do these days. One way to test the belief that everything is impossible is to start with relatively simple tasks and gradually increase the demand or break down complex tasks into smaller steps. This technique is referred to as *graded task assignment* (Beck, et al., 1979).

When breaking tasks down into manageable parts, don't expect yourself to do anything but one or two steps at a time toward completing tasks. If the house is a mess, a reasonable assignment for a depressed person would be to focus on sorting the laundry. Not washing, folding, ironing; just sorting. Tomorrow's task will be to wash and fold. Regarding the bills, a reasonable assignment for a depressed person would be to go and get stamps, or organize the unpaid bills. Regarding the work situation, reading the want ads in a newspaper or calling to inquire about a job would be reasonable.

You'll find that once you get moving a little with regard to your responsibilities, it's easier to continue moving, because you feel better. Don't set your expectations too high for starting things, especially things you've been avoiding or dreading for a while.

Planning and Engaging in Social Activities

First problem: "I'm in no condition to host a New Year's Eve party."

Response: Understandable. I'm suggesting small, brief social encounters. This can be having lunch with a friend, going to the zoo with your husband, talking on the phone with your cousin, or responding to e-mail.

Second problem: "My friends are busy; they can't be available every day."

Response: Socialization can simply be putting yourself in a social opportunity; that is, any situation where there is someone you can interact with. Even a grocery store is a social opportunity. There are other customers, there's the check out clerk, and there's the guy in the produce section spraying the veggies.

Don't overwhelm yourself with social encounters you're not currently equipped to do, like volunteering to host a televised political debate when you haven't spoken publicly in five years, because it might be a tad overwhelming and discouraging. Plan for social success, not more discouragement.

Some folks with depression have significant and/or longstanding problems in their ability to interact with others, or they have overwhelming social anxiety. If this is the case, it would be worthwhile for them to consult with a doctor about the adjunct benefit of medication or a therapist who is skilled in helping people increase and improve their socialization.

On the next page is an example of a completed Activity Planning and Monitoring Form.

When we review this very well documented day, we see definite ups and downs. There were times when this person was able to follow through with her plans, and times she didn't. There were times her predicted enjoyment was accurate, and plenty of times when it wasn't.

Activity Planning and Monitoring Form (Example)

	Planned Activity	Anticipated Pleasure	Actual Activity	Actual Pleasure	Thoughts
7	Wake up.	2	Woke up 7:30. Lay in bed until 8:00.	1	Everything is falling apart. I can't face the day. I can't call work today.
8	Eat breakfast.	3	Got up. Made some eggs. Was hungry after all.	5	Maybe there's some truth to the idea of putting the cart before the horse. Maybe I can get out of this.
9	Shower, dress, tidy up.	3	Showered, dressed, did a load of wash too.	7	Not bad. I haven't been able to get something accomplished in weeks.
10	Watch TV.	5	Worried about calling human resources.	2	I'll probably lose my job. They don't want me back. They probably think I'm a nut.
11	Call human resources, watch TV.	1	Scripted what I was to say. Went okay.	6	Whew. Thank goodness that's over. He was quite nice after all.
12	Watch TV.	5	Fell asleep until 1:30. Woke up feeling lousy.	2	Oh, this is never going to go away. I felt better before I went to sleep, but now I feel lousy again. It's useless.
1	Eat lunch.	3	Skipped lunch, watched TV.	3	I keep thinking about how I just can't go back to work. It's just awful.
2	Walk along the beach.	4	Walked along beach. Played with a dog, had conversation with a nice woman.	7	Maybe I'm not so repellent after all. I guess I could change jobs if it doesn't work out.
3	Stop at store.	2	Picked up stuff. Also went to post office to check box.	6	Not as many bills as I was expecting and avoiding.
4	Call best friend, invite for dinner.	6	Left message, looking forward to dinner.	7	This will be fun. I need some good company tonight.
5	Hopefully have friend over.	6	Friend called back. Had plans. Suggested tomorrow.	1	He doesn't care about me. What a loser I am. He has better things to do than hang around this sad slug.
6	Have dinner with friend.	6	Ate out of a can while standing in the kitchen staring at wall.	2	Still wondering if my friend is just blowing me off. I feel sick after eating such a meal.
7	Watch TV.	6	Tried to watch TV, don't remember show.	3	Still worrying about work, why my friend didn't come, and this endless depression.
8	Watch TV.	6	Went to sleep.	3	
9	Friend will leave. Clean up.	2	Slept.		
10	Take medicine, go to sleep.	2	Woke up. Couldn't sleep. Took nighttime medication.	2	I'm going to be taking these pills for the rest of my life.

Reviewing Your Schedule

There are several ways this exercise can pan out. Each is useful, even if you weren't able to do the things you planned.
 A. *Some of the activities I planned didn't happen.* Okay, could be you're trying to do too much. Lower your expectations to make the activities more doable. Or if the activities aren't too much, but you're feeling so miserable that it doesn't seem worth it, remind yourself that action comes before motivation when it comes to ballooning out of a depression. (Chapter Eight deals with motivation, and offers some tools for enhancing the drive to do things.) If your energy is so depleted by the depression that you are finding it impossible to get out of bed, you really should see your doctor, or make an appointment with a psychiatrist who can determine whether you need some prescription aid to get moving. Some folks are very, very depressed and absolutely need a pharmacological intervention before they will be capable of using the sort of tools we are discussing. If you are downright opposed to medicine and seeing a professional, then create an experiment for yourself. Give yourself several days or a week of trying to use the methods provided here. If your depression doesn't lift at all, then see a doctor. Remember, the trick is to get out of depression as quickly as possible. The longer it endures, the harder it is to break out of.
 B. *My predictions for pleasure are sometimes lower than what I actually derived from the activities. I consistently predict I'm going to have a rotten time, and sometimes I actually have a good time.* Hopefully, this will lead to your first "ah ha!" experience while implementing these exercises. Depression pollutes our predictions. Following through despite a miserable forecast can lead to surprisingly different outcomes. Now that you know that some activities can be enjoyable or at least less

depressing, start scheduling these sorts of activities regularly.

C. *My predictions of pleasure are fairly accurate, but I notice that when I prevent myself from withdrawing, I feel better and have more energy. It makes it easier to keep going, not crawl back into bed.* Great. Keep it up. Again, having seen this pan out in your own experience, you're in a position to seize the reins and start trying to prevent withdrawal tomorrow.

D. *My predictions for pleasure are sometimes higher than what I actually derive. I predicted that I'd get at least a seven out of walking the mall on Sunday, but I spent an hour and a half there, and I had a miserable time. Three was my rating of pleasure.* This is the purpose of the automatic thought monitoring column. If you've monitored your thoughts, you'll probably notice that when you are feeling the most depressed, your thoughts tend to be the worst. If, while strolling through the mall, you were thinking "Gee, what a wretched worm I am, strolling through the mall in the middle of the day. Look at all this merchandise the fortunate are able to afford. Look at the masses, laughing, chewing soft pretzels and paired off in love. Now look at me in the store window reflection. What a no good insect I am. I must be reeling in a couple vats of pity from the mall crowd today," it's no wonder you had a wretched time. This exercise can help you begin to see the intimate relationship between negative thinking and negative mood.

Now if you've given the activity monitoring and planning exercise a shot, I hope a case has been made that it is a necessary thing to keep doing. If not, give it a try. I suggest that you do so not only until your depression lifts, but for several weeks afterward. Depressed people don't tend to be very good self-monitors, so this skill is a good one to practice. Also, you're going to be sensitive to a relapse for a while, and it's a good thing to keep a reliable buffer in place.

Some folks get burned out on activity monitoring and planning and prematurely abandon it, or do it irregularly. One way of not allowing this important activity to be abandoned is to make a game out of it. The goal in this game is to spend as many hours as you can during any given day not being depressed. The more frequent the periods of brighter mood and the longer the periods of brighter mood, the closer you are to being the winner in terms of ridding yourself of this nasty mood state.

Depression doesn't come on suddenly; likewise, it doesn't just pop like a bubble. Recovery is generally linear, but rarely smooth. Don't miss the opportunity to reward yourself for small improvements. When you're depressed, it is a noteworthy accomplishment to have prepared dinner, read the paper, or decided not to languish the afternoon away in bed. Similarly, don't flagellate yourself or fall into a state of hopelessness because you had a bad day after a day of improvement. When you are rising from the depressive quagmire, you will have good days and bad days. Getting down on yourself only makes for an even more prolonged setback. The dips are opportunities to learn more and more about your unique depression, what environmental changes affect your mood negatively, and how intimately your thinking is connected to how you feel. The more you understand and the more success you have in rebounding from dips, the more resilient to depression you'll be.

Main Points

1. Mood varies throughout the day, and the variance corresponds to changes in attitude and behavior. If you're depressed, it is important for you to discover this in your own life. Plan and monitor your activity with some version of the Activity Planning and Monitoring Form to help you see the ups and downs in your day.
2. Brief batches of mood improvement are significant. They are periods during which the depression is losing

its strength. However, the weight of clinical depression is so heavy that the patches don't last. Getting out of depression involves creating more patches of relief by deliberately changing your thinking, stopping the behaviors that make your depression worse, and increasing activity that is reliably associated with improvements in your mood.

3. Recovery from depression is not smooth and linear. It is common for depressed people to make the normal lapses in their recovery seem much worse than they are. It is vital to keep hammering away at depression with continued structure, activity, and modification of your thinking.

Chapter Three:

Thinking about Thinking

Cognitive therapy is not simply relying on positive thinking, as is commonly believed. For depressed people to simply increase the number of happy self-statements like "Every day in every way I'm getting better and better," though perhaps perking mood for a few moments, doesn't tend to reduce depression. This is because the preponderance of negative automatic thoughts, beliefs, and memories runs contrary to such fluffy positive affirmations. They simply bounce off the rigorous depressive information processing system.

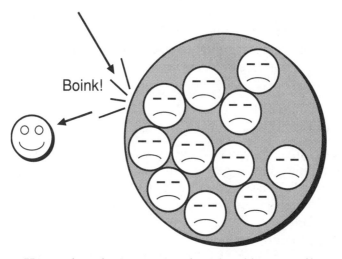

Happy thoughts are outnumbered and bounce off.

As stated by Phillip Kendall (1990), cognitive therapy is more about "non-negative" thinking. This may seem synonymous with positive thinking, but it isn't. Non-negative thinking requires the identification of negative thoughts and the modification of them such that they either become positive, or at least less negative.

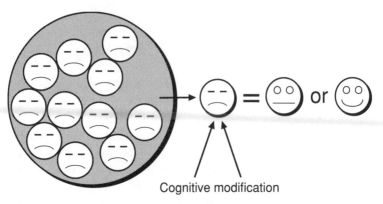

Cognitive modification

Negative thoughts are isolated and then subjected to scrutiny and modification.

Non-negative thinking is a considerably more difficult task for a depressed person, and the next three chapters will offer a variety of techniques for becoming more able to catch and alter negative thinking. First, though, let's look at something that makes our brains special, and particularly able to do this.

Meta What?

Cognitive change is about enhancing *metacognition*. This important sounding term simply means "thinking about thinking." When we mull over different options, evaluate our ideas, or edit our assumptions, we are engaging in metacognition.

Metacognition is one of our most evolved mental capabilities, and though quite mundane, is really amazing if you think about it (which, of course, would be thinking about thinking about thinking).

This advanced ability to be conscious of our own thoughts is something other animals don't possess. Imagine a snake thinking, "What was I just thinking about? Oh, yeah, whether that terrier would fit in my mouth. No, no; I've sworn off domestic pets, and I need to stick to my diet." That would be serpentine metacognition. Not likely. He'll

**Thinking about thinking is quite an extraordinary
ability . . . when you think about it.**

bare his teeth and secure his next meal, because that's what
his brain is hard wired to do in such situations.

Here's some human metacognition in action: Randy
comes home after a long brutal day, and after having sat in
traffic for an hour with a busted car stereo, he comes pushing through the screen door, seeing first that no one's even
started making dinner and that the kids' toys are strewn all
over. Randy's thinking, "This isn't fair! I've been working all
day, sitting in traffic, busted radio, etc., and things should be
calm and in order when I come home!" But then metacognition kicks in. Randy examines the automatic thought and
considers other information, such as the fact that his wife
has been with three young kids since before daybreak, and
is rightfully exhausted herself. All this tinkering with the
facts results in a new conclusion: "It's wrong for me to
expect dinner to be served and the house to be immaculate.
She's had a long hard day too." Randy proceeds inside,
gives his wife, Glenda, a big kiss, and says, "How about I
make dinner tonight?"

Without metacognition, that wouldn't have happened. Instead, Randy would have marched into the kitchen and started complaining about his chicken potpie not being ready. Metacognition saved Randy (and Glenda) from having a miserable night of arguments and indigestion.

It's like we have the option to let our thinking go on auto pilot, which we do 99 percent of the time, or to wake up this "other self," our metacognitive self, who, while the information processing system is still operating, can examine its operations and make alterations with regard to process and content if it seems advantageous to do so. It's a fail-safe mechanism for when habitual thinking is not panning out. Metacognition can get us out of bad loops like depression.

Redirecting Thought Process with Metacognition

In Chapter One, a distinction was made between *thought processes* and *thought products*. Thought processes are thinking actions, such as paying attention or retrieving a memory. *Thought product* refers to the stuff our thoughts are made of. I can try to remember an argument I had with my friend yesterday (which is a thought process), and after remembering the argument, I can have thoughts about what a loser I am for starting the argument (which is my thought content).

Let's look at strategies for gaining more control over our thought processes. The three thought processes we want to get a rein on are *attention, memory retrieval,* and *stream of consciousness (or mind-wandering)*. All are strongly influenced by depression, and, if unchecked, can strengthen and prolong it.

Negative Attentional Focus

When you're depressed, negative information in the environment sticks out more noticeably than neutral and positive information. It's harder to ignore negative stuff when you're depressed. Our attention, or focus, seems to hone in automatically on unpleasant things. It can literally seem like the whole world is turning into a toilet with a broken flusher. The newspaper is nothing but a journal of monsters and mayhem; the movie theatres host nothing but stories of loss and misery; the sidewalk is pregnant with wasted lives and meaningless strides. In reality, the world is no uglier than it has ever been, only it is capturing more of your attention at the expense of other neutral and positive stuff.

How does this focus on the negative worsen depression? Well, come sundown, what has your day been filled with? Just the negatives. Since negative information is capturing your attention, it is consequently being processed more deeply, taking up much of your waking cognitive space, and adding to the stockpile of depressing memories.

Try to deliberately stop this tendency to focus on the negative by:

- Forcing yourself to search out the positive and neutral information. In a specific situation, keep your attention from gravitating toward the negative by deliberately honing in on pleasant things. For example, if you're at the beach, focus on the curling waves, the people playing volleyball, and the children squealing and building sand castles, not the rotting seaweed, the dead gull, the sewage flowing into the sea, and the cigarette butts.

- Choosing activities and environments least likely to be construed as negative. Place yourself in environments where there are more stimuli that you would reckon as positive, for example, parks and nature preserves, as opposed to cemeteries and squalid parts of town. Not everyone likes parks and nature preserves, so think of places associated with positive times in your life. One person's theme park is another person's prison. For example, I like eucalyptus groves. I absolutely love the medicinal smell of the leaves, the sound of the crackling bark under my feet, the majestic height of the trees, and the pale, tranquil color of their trunks and limbs. I took a friend through one of my favorite groves once, and he didn't like it at all. He found it creepy, stinky, and foreboding.

• Selecting books, magazines, movies and videos most likely to distract from a negative mood. Depression seems to have a magnetism for gloomy novels, tragic movies, and melancholy tunes. Many people gravitate toward media that evoke a spectrum of emotions, including sadness, and when feeling okay can tolerate *Schindler's List,* or *Terms of Endearment,* or Mahler's *Ninth Symphony.* When you're depressed, the negative stuff can pull you down deeper. You may find that you need to take a break from such material until your depression lifts, and select films, books, and so on that are more uplifting.

Negative Self-Focused Attention

Depression creates an imbalance between outward-focused attention and self-focused attention (e.g., Smith & Greenberg, 1981). Depressed people are very self-focused, and it isn't the same thing as "selfish" or "conceited." Far from it. Depressed people are very self-absorbed and full of worry, spending inordinate time thinking about losses and defeat, and recycling thoughts about their symptoms and negative aspects of themselves and their circumstances. Negative self-focused attention worsens depression because the depressed person literally doesn't leave his or her head—and when someone is depressed, that person's head is a rotten place to spend a lot of time.

Prolonged periods of negative self-focused attention really feed depression. Distraction from the environment helps you keep a distance from the depression and thus weakens it. The longer you spend recycling negative events, worrying about things that make you depressed and other negative themes, the more voltage these networks of thinking gain. Consequently, they become harder and harder to stop. Further, a negatively self-focused mindset attaches here-and-now-events to those networks of information processing. Thus, if you worried about your losses the whole time you were at the grocery store, the next time you go, you will be compelled to worry about your losses again. The grocery store then becomes a depression trigger. What we think about, and consequently how we feel, is very situation dependent. The last thing we want to do is dirty up the beautiful landscape with more depression.

I've heard many depressed people say that they do a lot of journaling. There are right and wrong ways to journal when depressed. I believe that despite pop psychology lore, there is nothing inherently medicinal about journaling. Most journaling I've seen from depressed people tends to be unbridled wordings of what's going on in their depressed heads; grueling miserable dissertations of hopelessness, helplessness and worthlessness. Here's an example of a young fellow's journal entry he shared with the cognitive depression group one dark and freezing January morning:

"Today is dark and cold. Like my life. I have nothing to live for. Everything I've done has eventually turned into failure. Nobody likes me. I should live in a cave."

With a big frown on his face he said that he'd read somewhere that venting your feelings like that will make you feel better. Then he admitted that after he was finished journaling he usually drew the curtains down and crawled into bed. When you're depressed, reviewing negative material just makes the negative material more real in your mind, and in effect, makes you feel worse. Journaling for the sake of journaling when you're depressed can increase negative self-absorption. Later, we'll look at a good substitute to journaling, in which you will not only monitor your thinking, but be able to catch and correct errors and distortions that contribute to your depression.

Here are some other tips to help you decrease self-focused attention:

- Work toward getting as absorbed in activities as possible. Try to keep your attention from going inward by trying to take part in all aspects of your environment. Thought stopping is a simple cognitive tool for worriers.

Develop a cue word or image to activate when you notice negative self-focused attention. Create your own stop sign, or the use a command such as "Knock it off," (to be uttered only in your thoughts, of course). Try to make experiences as multi-sensory as possible.

- Stop comparing. Depressed people make far too many self-comparisons. A room of people becomes an opportunity to compare all your failures to their (perceived) successes and strengths. Use the thought stopping method to bring this activity to a halt. A cue word or phrase, such as "Stop comparing!" that you can say to yourself whenever you catch yourself doing this can be helpful. Then, switch to some other mental topic. Repeated use of cue words can "train your brain" to alert you automatically.

- Choose activities every day that demand a lot of attention. Examples would be social activities in which you need to interact, hobbies such as playing an instrument, video games, roaming the internet, puzzles, and very interesting fiction and videos.

- Look outside yourself. When you're alone, it is more difficult to remain outwardly focused. Therefore, create mental activities involving outside stimuli. For example, if you are driving, try to "figure out" or guess the occupations of the people who pass you, brainstorm about what would improve the landscapes you pass, or look for shapes in cloud formations.

- Create positive self-focused attention. Sometimes, such as waking up in the wee hours, it is impossible to be anything but self-focused. This doesn't mean the tone has to be negative, however. Use alone time for unbridled positive fantasy, thinking vividly about aspects of yourself *not* influenced by depression; brainstorm, without restraint, for ways to improve your lot; or think about career changes, vacations, learning new skills, and first novel ideas. Basically, let yourself have the sort of zany flights of imagination that occur when you're not depressed.

Negative Memory Retrieval and Mind-Wandering

When people are depressed, negative memories seem to be waiting just below the surface to jump up and invade consciousness. Based on the work of Gordon Bower (1981) and others, Rick Ingram suggested that when we're depressed, "networks" of depressive memories become "activated" (Ingram, 1984). Depressed people tend to isolate themselves and consequently don't have many distractions. Therefore, the negative memories tend to bubble and pop into their awareness with ease. Depressed people—especially when alone—will find themselves regurgitating negative memory after negative memory, both recent and distant. Plus, situations even remotely resembling negative events of the past will dredge up more negative memories. A depressed person may be watching a film, and based on a scene vaguely referring to death, find himself thinking about his mom's death, his grandfather's death, or his dog's death.

A person's stream of consciousness, which is the linking of one idea to another, always ends up in the gutter when he's depressed. He could be driving alone, see an orange sign, then begin thinking about pumpkins, then start recall-

Negative self-focused attention can really sink a conversation.

ing Halloweens of bygone days, which takes him to reviewing other holidays. After a few minutes of mind-wandering,
Valentine's Day pops into his mind, linked to a failed relationship, and eventually he is into a mindset of hopelessness
with regard to ever having a lasting intimate relationship.
And to think that the color orange triggered all that!
Instead, that person should practice using distraction (a
very underrated metacognitive tool) and redirection of
thought to keep his mind from wandering off the road and
ending up in the slough so much.

Some tips for countering negative memory retrieval and
mind-wandering include:

- Don't let yourself dwell on things that make you depressed. Sometimes it is helpful, especially with anxious depression, to postpone worry. To do that, set aside
  a half-hour slot later in the day to worry and recycle
  negative memories without censure, but forbid yourself
  to dwell on such memories at any other time in the day.
- Deliberately conjure up memories from better times.
  Though the negative ones will continuously try to interfere, practice pulling from the mothballs of your memory events from the recent and distant past not associated with loss, rejection, defeat, powerlessness, and the
  like.
- Choose environments, situations, and people likely to
  cause you to bring up positive memories. Avoid spending a lot of time in spots associated with a very
  depressed mood. Sometimes this is not completely possible, as homes or workplaces are often associated with
  the worst levels of depression. If this is the case, consider changing the layout of rooms most associated
  with profound depression. For example, if you've spent
  a lot of time in bed during the deepest period of your
  depression, consider reorganizing the furniture in your
  room, even changing the direction of your bed. When
  an aspect of the environment, even a piece of furniture,
  is strongly associated with depression, it can possess
  the strength to remind you vividly (and emotionally) of

it. Changing the environment, even subtly, can weaken this tendency.

These recommendations for altering cognitive process may seem to be pretty much common sense, but they are much more difficult in practice than they appear in print. Try to do them as often as you can. Remember, recovery from depression is patchy. The more periods, even brief periods, of relief you can foster by changing your behavior and thinking, the weaker the depression becomes, until it eventually breaks completely.

Main Points

1. Depression exerts a powerful effect on our thinking. In addition to confusion, poor concentration, memory impairment, and distractibility, the flavor of our thinking becomes generally negative and morbidly self-focused.

2. Simply relying on positive thinking, a common recommendation in the popular press, is not going to have a tremendous effect on your thoughts when you are depressed. This is because perky little self-statements like "I'm a good person" are quickly outnumbered in our minds, which are monopolized by negativity when we're depressed.

3. Non-negative thinking, that is, identifying and altering negative thoughts, is much more powerful in terms of reducing depression than the just trying to think about positive thoughts. However, this exercise is much more difficult, mostly because it is hard to concentrate if you are depressed.

4. Metacognition means "thinking about thinking." It is a uniquely human ability that enables us to check our automatic thoughts and beliefs for accuracy.

5. Attention, memory retrieval, and stream of consciousness are all negatively influenced by depression. It is important to use distraction and to redirect thinking frequently, as these symptoms tend to strengthen depression.

Chapter Four:

Testing Gloomy Data: The Thought Record Flow Sheet

Chapter Three offered some ways to gain control over depressive thinking, such as distracting yourself from the recycling of negative memories, changing the direction of your stream of consciousness, and redirecting attention away from the self. Now it's time to focus on the content of thoughts themselves. There are a number of techniques that can be used when depressive thoughts are identified so that more balanced, realistic interpretations can be discovered. Cognitive therapy techniques are simple in theory but require a lot of practice.

In the next two chapters, we will look at a variety of methods for catching and changing negative thoughts. Some of them require paper and pencil, some you can do in your head.

Thought Content Equals Mood Content

Before we delve into these techniques, it is important for you to understand the relationship between our thoughts and our feelings. Our moods change all the time, but we usually don't give much credit to the role our thoughts play in this process. We blame "things happening," not how we are conceptualizing the things that happen. Consider Jill, a young law student who is dating a very enterprising gentleman named Jack. Their relationship was running smoothly until one day, Jack broke up with Jill. Jill was devastated. She crawled into bed, started skipping her classes, and in a week's time, she was steeped in depression.

If we ask Jill why she's so depressed, she'll probably say, "Because Jack broke up with me." Most people would join Jill in coming to the conclusion that mood is directly influenced by environmental changes.

If we ask Jill what she's been thinking about all holed up there in her bedroom, she might say, "It's all my fault. I snarl up everything I touch. I'll never have a lasting positive relationship. What a loser I am." Jill might qualify her thoughts by adding, "You'd be thinking this way too if you'd been dumped," as though her miserable thoughts are a byproduct of having broken up and feeling depressed.

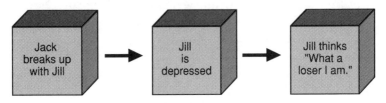

Most people think mood is caused by events.

To challenge this sequence, let's imagine that instead of having those self-critical and hopeless thoughts, Jill is thinking, "Oh, my gosh! I'm all alone, and I can't stand it! I'll be squashed by the mean world without Jack. I can't cope with all the horror in my life without Jack! What am I going to do?" Somehow, I don't reckon Jill would be depressed, nor would she be angry. She'd be highly anxious, shaking and hyperventilating, calling her family to come and get her.

Or, suppose Jill is thinking, "That no good, two-timing jerk used me! He had no right to lead me on like this. He's completely messed up my life and tried to make me look like a fool in front of my friends." If Jill were thinking this way, it is unlikely that she'd be lying in a pool of depression; rather, she'd be full of anger and tearing up his love letters.

Believe it or not, this kindergarten-simple concept has enormous implications. It suggests that mood is dependent on how we think, not on what happens to us. Of course, there are some events, such as tragic events, in which you would not find much variance in terms of people's emotional reactions, but even events such as a death or a divorce can result in very different emotional responses depending on how the event is construed.

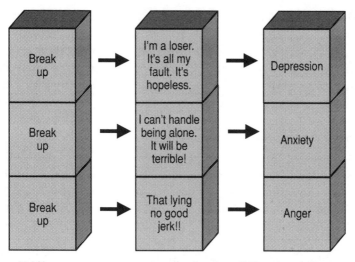

Different responses to events lead to different results.

We are constantly thinking, and most of the time we don't put a great deal of effort into addressing the logic of our thoughts. We just trust them to be sound and reliable. In order for cognitive techniques to work for you, you have to practice them every day. Every time you identify a distorted thought and modify it, you have strengthened a new way of thinking, which can eventually become automatic. Each time you miss out, or ignore a distorted thought, you strengthen old ways. Does this mean that you will be forced to scrutinize every thought that enters your mind for the rest of your life? Of course not; this would make anyone crazy! The key is to implement cognitive skills where the distortions lie. Few people think erroneously all the time. The more effort you put into practicing cognitive techniques in high-risk situations, the less risky they will become.

The Thought Record Flow Sheet

The bread and butter of cognitive therapy has always been the Thought Record. Aaron Beck and his colleagues initially developed the Daily Record of Dysfunctional Thoughts, or

DRDT (Beck et al., 1979). I've sampled many creative adaptations over the years. The goal of the thought record is to learn how to catch and alter the negative thoughts that contribute to depression. In this chapter, I've attempted to make the exercise as easy and potentially fruitful as possible. The Thought Record Flow Sheet we're going to look at was reported by my patients to be the most straightforward and easy to use of the several versions sampled.

It's hard to concentrate when you're depressed, and motivation is often almost completely wound down. I've found in treating depressed patients that an overly involved paper and pencil exercise will often be shunned or it will be done incorrectly. This can lead to discouragement, which doesn't help depression.

When I present the Thought Record Flow Sheet to patients, usually the first question they ask is how often they should do this exercise. My answer is to do this as often as they can. Some therapists tell patients to try to do one a day, but one a day probably won't cut it. Plus, telling a depressed person to do a very important exercise once a day conveys the idea that it really isn't that important. Yeah, sure, there are some things where once a day is sufficient, such as waking up, showering, taking your vitamin complex, but once a day for the Thought Record Flow Sheet isn't enough, especially if that is all someone does in the course of a day to exercise metacognition. I suggest that you try to complete at least four or five flow sheets per day. Photocopy a few dozen of the sheets so you'll always have a blank one handy.

The best time to complete the Thought Record Flow Sheet (TRFS) is when you notice your mood worsening. When you're depressed it's ugly most of the time, but even so, there are times when it sinks further. This is the prime time to use this technique, as you will see most strikingly the effect of metacognition on falling mood.

However, times of worsening mood do not always lend themselves to paper and pencil tasks. For example, if you

The Thought Record Flow Sheet

1. Emotion

(Rate level of depression)

depression_____%

2. Situation Causing the Emotion

3. Big Bad Thought

What does the situation say about <u>me</u>, <u>my control</u>, or <u>my future?</u>

4. Evidence the Thought Is 100% True

5. Dr. Frankenstein Technique: Build Someone or Some Situation to Which the Thought Would Apply Completely.

6. Evidence That the Thought Is Not 100% True

7. New, More Accurate Thought

8. Re-Rating of Emotion

depression_____%

are driving through the winding eucalyptus grove and your mood is sinking, it would not be a good idea to whip out a TRFS and start metacognating there over the steering wheel. Nor would it be appropriate to be in the midst of a volatile no-winner with your boss and suddenly leave the room and do a TRFS.

Try to complete a thought record as close to the time of your mood slump as possible. You can still benefit if several hours have passed. In fact, with most depressed folks, the thoughts they dispute are the same thoughts that crop up time and time again. So if you miss the chance when you're crossing six lanes of traffic, don't worry; chances are, you'll get another chance.

Some people will simply schedule various times in the day to sit down and do a thought record. I think this is a good plan, given how unstructured time just seems to get sucked right into the dark bedroom. On your activity monitoring and planning form, schedule in time to do some thought records, especially during times when your depression seems to be the most heavy.

The Thought Record Flow Sheet: Step by Step

Let's take a tour through the completion of a successful thought record. You may think something like this shouldn't take so many pages to explain, but remember, this is a new exercise for most people. It doesn't matter if you've been doing long division and calculus functions in your head or litigating victoriously through each and every disagreement prior to getting depressed; metacognition is very brain intensive when you're bogged down by depression.

Step 1. Rate your depression on a scale of 0 to 100%, based on previous experience with the emotion (100 = most extreme depression ever experienced, 0 = complete absence of depression).

There are two reasons for rating mood at this point. First, since the TRFS is a test per se, we want a "pre" rating, which is a measure of mood before you do the TRFS, and a "post" rating, which is a measure of mood after you've done the TRFS. It can be very encouraging to see your ratings diminish as you do Thought Record Flow Sheets. This will usually lead to another one of those very much desired "ah ha!" experiences.

Everyone is different in terms of their experience with depression, as well as tolerance of negative emotions. What I rate as 75% depressed you might rate as 65%, or vice versa. Create your own personalized barometer of mood to compare your current state with.

First, think about a time your depression was at its worst and rate this as 100%. That terrible time may have been associated with a tremendous loss or defeat, or associated with severe depressive symptoms, such as suicidal thoughts. A rating of 75% would represent a time you were very depressed, but not quite as badly as with the event that earned 100%. A rating of 50% might correspond to an event leading to depressed mood, but not to the extent that you completely checked out. You might consider 25% to be one of the typical crummy events we all encounter daily, like dealing with a rude clerk, opening a larger than expected utility bill, or accidentally stepping into the rain filled gutter. This gets you in a grumpy mood, but it is not enough to impede your stride. Zero percent, of course, would be a situation in which there was no depression at all. Using this mood gauge, assign a percentage score based on how you feel right now.

1. Emotion
(Rate level of depression)
depression **75**%

Step 2. Identify the situation associated with your mood deteriorating. What is going right now such that you are feeling worse? Be *objective* here—stick to the facts of the event, as a newspaper article might describe them. Examples of events described objectively might be "I turned in my report a day late," or "My boss scolded me," or "I had

an argument with my spouse," or "My friend forgot my birthday." Those are statements of fact.

However, saying, "I totally messed up my life again," would not be an example of an objective rendering. This is a vast catastrophic generalization about some event, and it belongs in the next box, the Big Bad Thought box. That's where we put *subjective* thoughts; that is, how we think about something.

Separating objective and subjective descriptions is hard for some folks, who are used to fusing their attributions with the facts as though they are inseparable. This step alone can be helpful for depressed people, when they have to view the events about which they are feeling terrible in their innocent nakedness.

Sometimes mood just sinks and nothing is going on. You may be sitting there on the couch watching a talk show and your mood is rotting like a dead fish. There's nothing inherently depressing about the talk show; in fact, you may not even be paying attention to it.

2. Situation Causing the Emotion
Breaking up with girlfriend.

Why does mood just sink sometimes? Though the biochemistry of depression can create fluctuations, such as the way many people with depression feel their worst in the morning, the deterioration that seems to come out of nowhere is often due to the fact that the depressed person is cognitively gnawing some nasty topic. For example, I may be awake at three in the morning, doing absolutely nothing, but I've elected to use this time to ponder my father's untimely death and our unresolved conflict, think about my marital problems, worry about work, and think about how long I've been depressed.

Remember, even though these topics are in essence cognitive, they are not in and of themselves causing you to be depressed. It is the angle you are putting on these topics and the unique meaning you are assigning them.

Consider the example above. If the topic associated with my mood worsening is "Thinking about how long I've been depressed," and I've rated my depression at 75%, a thick, dense scoop of depression, I'm probably having thoughts like, "I'll never get out of this, I'm a loser, and my wife is going to leave me." But now imagine if I had the same topic, which was thinking about how long I've been depressed, but I had rated my depression at only 15%, which is very little depression. This time, I would probably be having thoughts like, "Yes, I've been depressed for a long time, but I just started a new medication, and I think this cognitive stuff might help me finally get out of it. I've noticed an increase in patches of relief since I started structuring my days differently."

2. Situation Causing the Emotion
Thinking about how long I've been depressed.

Step 3. Now comes one of the more difficult parts of the Thought Record Flow Sheet, identifying the Big Bad Thought. Why is this part so hard? It's hard because, first of all, it isn't natural to pick out automatic thoughts from our experience. Furthermore, we don't think of thoughts as thoughts. They're just mixed into the whole of experience; they don't feel like a separate component of experience. As we meander through life, thoughts are being birthed at mosquito rate. Plus, we are parallel processing organisms; that is, many independent levels of thinking are occurring at the same time.

One common error people make with the Flow Sheet is to write an exhaustive list of automatic thoughts they're having. Billy was feeling depressed one day and decided to do a Thought Record Flow Sheet; here's what he wrote in the Big Bad Thought box:

No, sorry; you get one thought per record. Just one. And it has to be the worst one of all; the ugliest, slinkiest, most miserable thought currently occurring in your parallel processing brain, or an ugly summary thought which best depicts the numerous putrid ideas occurring in your parallel processing brain. We want to identify only the thought responsible

> *I feel terrible. I wonder if Jackie will call tonight. Gee, this TV sure has a crummy picture. I can't even afford to upgrade that. Maybe I'll quit my job. Nobody likes me anymore. Jackie won't call, I'm certain of it. What's that on my shoe? Oh, man, I stepped in some gum; story of my life.*

for your mood being so awful. Now, sometimes you can put your finger on it immediately. For example, in response to a break up, I might be steeped in self-blame and self-loathing, and be able to identify, "I'm unlovable" right away.

If you're unsure whether you've found the Big Bad Thought, list some of the worst thoughts you are having, and then pick the winner. If you are thinking, "I'm going to be alone all weekend" and "It's impossible for me to make friends," the latter is obviously the more extreme of the two.

Do a quality check on your thought record so far. Ask

---

3. Big Bad Thought
What does the situation say about <u>me</u>, <u>my control</u>, or <u>my future</u>?

I'm unloveable.

---

yourself if it would it be reasonable for anyone to feel as bad as you do right then if they were having this thought. If the answer is yes, you've probably found a Big Bad Thought; if not, you need to go deeper. Further, you may be having a recurring image or something like your own tiny, miserable movie going through your mind. In response to a break up, you may be consumed with the image of your lost love or constantly reviewing the good old times. You won't be able to do a flow sheet on an image. Another problem is that you may be thinking a thought that is undisputable. Below, in response to a break up, you may be thinking, "She doesn't want to be with me anymore." You may get nowhere trying

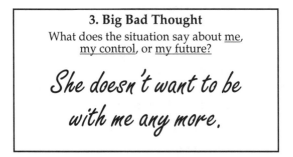

3. Big Bad Thought
What does the situation say about <u>me</u>,
<u>my control</u>, or <u>my future</u>?

She doesn't want to be with me any more.

to dispute this thought, as it might be a grim fact. It might be something she actually said to you 37 times, faxed to you, scratched it on the side of your car with a key, and sent her big brother over to remind you. How then, can you determine which Big Bad Thought to debate?

David Burns, M.D.(1980) coined what is called the Downward Arrow Technique. That technique has become a standard procedure in cognitive therapy. With this technique, patients can identify a deeper level of depressive thinking by asking themselves the implications of their negative automatic thoughts. For example, if I have a negative automatic thought like "I'm all alone," using the downward arrow technique, a therapist might ask me, or I can ask myself, what it means for me to be all alone. In reply, I might say, "I'm worthless and completely undesirable," which would certainly qualify as a "bigger and badder" thought than "I'm all alone."

Another technique, which many patients have reported to be very easy and reliable, to help you capture the nastiest of your thoughts is simply to ask what the situation you've identified would say about three important areas: your self, your control, and your future. Remember, worthless, helpless, and hopeless thoughts are the ones keeping you down. These are the ones you want to test.

Using the example of the break up, I can quickly discover three Big Bad Thoughts by asking myself:

1. What would this break up say about me?
   Possible answer: "I'm unlovable."
2. What would this break up say about my control over my intimate life?
   Possible answer: "I can't make relationships last."
3. What would this break up say about the possibility of my finding a lasting positive relationship in the future?
   Possible answer: "I'll never have a positive, lasting intimate relationship."

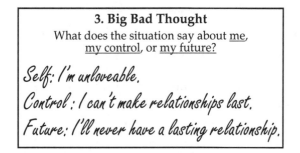

3. Big Bad Thought
What does the situation say about <u>me</u>,
<u>my control</u>, or <u>my future</u>?

Self: I'm unloveable.

Control: I can't make relationships last.

Future: I'll never have a lasting relationship.

When you're depressed, at least one component of the self-control-future trio is always active. You can't be depressed and not have hopeless, helpless or worthless thoughts brewing. When you assess these areas using this modified downward arrow, the Big Bad Thought will come leaping out of your brain and into your consciousness. If you've responded with a Big Bad Thought to all three cognitive triad areas, choose the worst of the three Big Bad Thoughts. Too many rotten thoughts listed on one thought record form can make the exercise overwhelming. And remember, sometimes successfully disputing one of a handful of bad thoughts can make the rest disappear for a while.

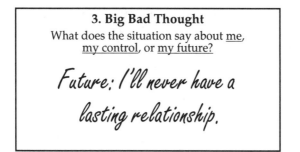

3. Big Bad Thought
What does the situation say about <u>me</u>,
<u>my control</u>, or <u>my future</u>?

Future: I'll never have a
lasting relationship.

Step 4. Next, list all evidence that supports the thought as accurate. What can you think of that backs up this Big Bad Thought? This is a particularly easy step in the thought record process, as the "evidence" is what keeps wheeling around your skull all day.

As with Step 2, identifying the situation, you can only put objective facts in this box. What facts do I believe support the Big Bad Thought? If my Big Bad Thought is "I'm unlovable" and I list as evidence that I'm ugly, I'm stupid, and I'm repellent, then I'm simply dumping more big bad thoughts on myself. Falling out with a friend, an argument with my mother, or a history of short-term relationships might be examples of facts I am using to support my negative self-assessment.

> **4. Evidence the Thought Is 100% True**
>
> *Recent break up.*
> *History of short-term relationships. I'm 42.*
> *Longest relationship only lasted three months. I'm very emotionally dependent.*

Important!

I must insert an important caveat at this point. Don't abandon the TRFS right now or you'll likely feel worse! I've seen so many depressed people get to this step and then discontinue that I've probably lost valuable hairs. Often people will feel a bit worse after this step, which makes sense, because they've just done an inventory on all the reasons they feel so miserable. At this point, the

thought record flow sheet seems like an exercise you'd want to avoid. But if you put it down now, this response will be reinforced, and you will be less likely to pick up another, thus missing the opportunity to see if this exercise works for you. Now, pick up that pen and trudge though the rest of the exercise.

Step 5. Step 5 involves listing evidence that refutes the Big Bad Thought; that is, listing any facts that argue that the thought is not 100% true. This is the hardest step of all. It is so difficult that, I believe, many people abandon the thought record technique as unhelpful because they are unable to come up with anything to put in this box. And it has nothing to do with poor motivation or low intelligence. My goodness, if I'm immersed in gloom, thinking about how I've messed up everything I've touched, the last thing I'm going to be able to do easily is come up with arguments against those claims.

The spectrum of depressive symptoms presented in Chapter One bears down on you when you come to this step. So I've come up with an intermediary step, one I've termed the Dr. Frankenstein Technique. It works like this: Take your Big Bad Thought, which in this example is, "I'll never have a lasting positive intimate relationship," and create, on the slab, just like Dr. Frankenstein did, a monster. However, your monster has to be one to which this thought would apply 100%. That monster would be a truly hopeless case. But that is *not you*!

The primary function of this exercise is to get you away from your self-absorption and to get you to see the thought from another vantage point; one in which the thought has been taken to its absurd face value. If you were going to build someone completely incapable of having an intimate relationship, someone so hopelessly alone that each and every observer would accept the thought that this person would never have a positive relationship, what characteristics would that person/monster you created have?

A. As you list attributes of your monster, pay attention to aspects of you and your situation that come to mind which are not like the monster you've created. In the example

5. Dr. Frankenstein Technique: Build Someone or Some Situation to Which the Thought Would Apply Completely.	6. Evidence That the Thought Is Not 100% True
A "monster" with no capacity for a long-term relationship would be selfish, irresponsible, devoid of social skills, appallingly ugly, without friends, without any relationship history, incapable of attracting people, uninterested in making change.	*I have friends, I attract people, I am not shy, I've been able to keep friends going for years (had best friend since grade school), I am loyal and faithful to people, I'm getting help for my dependency problems, other people 42 find relationships.*

below, a hopeless monster was created who would have no capacity for long-term relationships. Countering that idea is the presence of long-term friendships possessed.

B. Jot the countering evidence down as it comes to mind (quickly, before you discount it) in the box labeled Evidence That the Thought Is Not 100% True.

C. Pay attention to your mood as you complete these two steps. Usually, people will notice that they are feeling somewhat better.

Step 6. Now that we've found evidence that refutes the Big Bad Thought, we must replace the Big Bad Thought with one that is more accurate. The replacement thought is usually longer than the Big Bad Thought (Big Bad Thoughts tend to be short and either/or, black or white, concise negative generalizations; whereas accurate thoughts tend to be more detailed). Do not substitute the Big Bad Thought with a Pollyanna-like piece of nonsense thought like, "Every day in every way I'm getting better and better." The replacement thought does not have to be positive; it just has to be more accurate, which is usually less negative. Thinking that "I'm on the road to the most beautiful lasting relationship in the world" would be as distorted as the Big Bad Thought. Below, the replacement thought suggests that I have the capacity to have a good lasting relationship if I make some changes, which will take some work, but are worth it. There is nothing Pollyanna-like about this thought. It is realistic, pragmatic, and hopeful.

Step 7. The last step of the thought record is to re-rate your level of depression. Think back to your depression barometer. Does your mood feel any better? If so, how much? Usually, people will report 10, 20, or 30 percentage point drops in depression when they've done the

7. New, More Accurate Thought
I have a lot of what it takes to have a lasting relationship. I'm going to need to approach relationships differently if this is going to happen.

thought record correctly. Now this may seem like a drop in the bucket, but hold on. Think about what just occurred. Depression, the king of misery, was influenced, not by some miraculous change in your situation, but simply by tinkering with your thinking!

Savor that concept for a while, because it is truly amazing. The ability to have even a brief, moderate mood improvement based solely on metacognition suggests that depression has a weak spot, an Achilles' heel.

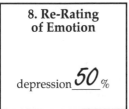

8. Re-Rating of Emotion
depression _50_ %

Remember, recovery from depression is patchy. The successfully completed thought record can create a period of relief, but one thought record will not break a depression. You need to do the thought record regularly. The more often you do the thought record, the longer the patches of relief will be, and the more able you will be to utilize the technique in your head.

Main Points

1. The thought record is a time-tested technique that will help you get out of depression.
2. Many people find a thought record hard to do; the step-by-step instructions given here are easier. So at least try it.
3. Do at least five thought records per day.
4. The sequence for a Thought Record Flow Sheet is as follows:
   a. Rate the level of depression.
   b. Identify situation related to current worsening mood.
   c. Identify the Big Bad Thought: Ask yourself what this situation would say about your self, your control over important areas, and your future.
   d. Do a quality check on the thought record so far; that is, ask yourself if anyone else would be this miserable if they believed this thought. List evidence that the Big Bad Thought is true. Remember, don't give up now, even if you are feeling worse.
   e. List evidence against the Big Bad Thought. Also, using the Dr. Frankenstein Technique, create someone or some situation for which your Big Bad Thought would be completely true. Then, list aspects of you and your situation that are not like the monster you've created.
   f. Write a balanced replacement thought for the Big Bad Thought.
   g. Re-rate your level of depression.

Chapter Five:

Derailing Depression's
One-Track Mind

The more, the better when it comes to using metacognition. The Thought Record Flow Sheet is like whacking Richard's ogre with a eucalyptus log. A successfully completed Thought Record Flow Sheet, that is, one after which you feel noticeably better, can leave the depressive ogre dizzying in the gutter for a half hour or more.

The Thought Record Flow Sheet exercise is hard to do when you're depressed, and if you are able to do the recommended five per day, it is a great accomplishment. However, I believe that doing even five thought records a day doesn't maximize metacognition's full capacity in terms of breaking your depression.

In this chapter, I'll offer some easier methods for enhancing metacognition, methods that aren't as labor intensive as the thought record, sort of like a variety of ball peen hammers to add to your heavy-duty sledgehammer. First we'll look at the Thought Debate Technique, which is another pencil and paper exercise, then we'll look at a variety of cognitive tricks you can do in your head.

The ultimate goal of cognitive behavior therapy is for you to be able to reliably hold the reins of your thinking. That way, you can catch and redirect automatic information processing that is feeding your depression and talk convincingly to yourself so that you realize your depressive thinking is not true.

The test of evidence of the Thought Record Flow Sheet is one way to exercise metacognition, but it is by no means the most natural. Natural metacognition is more like talking to yourself. When we're not depressed, it's much easier to converse with ourselves at a metacognitive level. For example, I may be in a fine mood, sitting here reading a book on the beach, debating whether to go into the water or finish the chapter. However, when we're depressed, there is one all-pervading mindset: negativity. Also, our strength to override that mindset is diminished. These exercises are designed to make metacognition easier during a time when talking yourself out of negative ideas isn't coming naturally.

The Thought Debate

The Thought Debate is a pencil and paper task that is considerably easier and faster to complete than the Thought Record Flow Sheet. There is no rating of your mood or testing of the evidence; rather, the Thought Debate flows more like natural metacognition. In fact, it's so easy and quick it shouldn't be a problem for you to do at least *four times as many* thought debates as flow sheets. That would be 20 a day at least, added to the five flow sheets you're already doing.

You may be thinking all this pencil and paper stuff is a bit schoolish, unlike the material in the more inspirationally oriented self-help books you've heard of or actually read. The exercises may have an academic feel; but, as I've stressed several times, depressions often lift quicker when people start thinking and behaving differently.

Cognitive disputation is like any new skill. You have to practice it to get good at it. You may have some inherent metacognitive talent, as an artist may have inherent painting ability, but you still have to practice. A talented artist will continue to push himself to improve his craft. So, whip out the pencils and let's get to torturing that ogre some more. Copy the Thought Debate form onto a sheet of paper or photocopy the one from the book. Just like the thought record, the best time to do a thought debate is when you notice your mood worsening. Or if you are an orderly sort, you can schedule them into your planner.

Document the time of day when you do the thought debate.

   1. Document what is occurring; that is, what's happening that is making your mood worse?

Thought Debate Record

Instructions: When you recognize that your mood is depressed, record the time of day, what is going on, the cognitive theme or themes, and the automatic thought in line with the themes. Debate or argue with the automatic thought as though you were taking the side of someone who didn't believe the thought to be completely true. Then record the result of the debate—if you feel better, feel worse, or feel the same.

Time	Situation	Theme	Big Bad Thoughts	Debate/Argument	Result
		Hopeless Helpless Worthless			
		Hopeless Helpless Worthless			
		Hopeless Helpless Worthless			
		Hopeless Helpless Worthless			

69

2. Examine the cognitive triad in the third box: *hopeless,
   helpless* and *worthless*. Find the Big Bad Thought by asking yourself if your current mindset is in line with any
   of these three themes. By the way, if you're depressed,
   at least one of the cognitive triad themes is occurring.
   You can't be feeling morbidly depressed without having hopelessness, helplessness or worthlessness thriv-
   ing in your head. Use the cognitive triad as three
   meshed cognitive filters. Believe me, when you sweep
   them through your thinking, you'll notice a lot of cognitive crud left in the filters.
3. When one of the cognitive triad themes finds a match,
   it will holler out to you. Your thoughts might go something like this: "Hmmm, am I having hopeless
   thoughts about my friend not calling? No. Hmmm,
   how about helplessness? No, I feel pretty much in control right now. Is it worthlessness? BINGO! Holy Moly!
   I'm a friendless loser! Nobody likes me!"

With hopelessness, the word "never" has usually settled
in. Thoughts like "It's never going to get better," or "My life
is over," or "Future pleasure in my life is impossible," may
take over your thinking. When helplessness is operating,
you will often discover the presence of the word "can't" in
your brain, or the word "impossible" will raise its hand. The
idea of "powerless" usually is discovered standing and shiv-
ering next to the temporal lobe (the part of our brain that
houses our response center for fear). When worthlessness is
depression's current theme, you may identify thoughts like,"
I'm no good, I'm a failure, and I totally messed up my life."

You may find that more than one theme is operating. Pick
the one that seems the most terrible and circle it. If you feel
two or three are currently operating, often successfully
debating one will make you feel better. You don't necessarily have to do two or three more thought debates. If you still
feel miserable after doing the thought debate, however, it
may be that you did not choose the true cognitive culprit. So
in this case, do another.

4. Write down the Big Bad Thought in your own words. As with the thought record, keep it concise. You get one simple sentence, not a four-paragraph journal entry.
5. Then move on to the argument box. Here, I want you to take the thought on as though it has provoked you. Debate it. Argue with it. Discount it. Pretend you are a "Lawyer of mind" and that thought on the witness stand is a big liar who's about to get exposed. Don't hold back. Write a convincing disputation of the ugly thought you've identified, all the while attending to your mood. Does it improve as you litigate? Stay the same? Worsen? Does it improve briefly with some ideas, then get worse with others? Really pay attention to how your thought and your mood dance with each other. Thought is usually taking the lead, with mood stumbling clumsily in tow.

Many of you will find that once you know what you need to be arguing, you are good litigators after all. When you're depressed, it's hard to sense that the idea that you are lovable is swimming around in all that sorrow and woe. Once you put it under a strong light, it becomes an entity. It's something to challenge. So challenge it.

For some people, argumentation is not their main strength. You can be a perfectly intelligent person and not necessarily have a knack for belaboring political rhetoric into the evening. Some don't like to argue. That's cool. Some people do fine staying away from arguments with others. However, you need to learn how to argue with yourself and win if you're going to get out of this depressive mood. Below are seven methods of thought debate. Not all of them apply to each and every Big Bad Thought, but I want you to practice them all. These are simply methods of stepping away from a depressive thought enough to see it from a rational perspective and to challenge it.

Thought Debate Record (Example)

Instructions: When you recognize that your mood is depressed, record the time of day, what is going on, the cognitive theme or themes, and the automatic thought in line with the themes. Debate or argue with the automatic thought as though you were taking the side of someone who didn't believe the thought to be completely true. Then record the result of the debate—if you feel better, feel worse, or feel the same.

Time	Situation	Theme	Big Bad Thoughts	Debate/Argument	Result
8 A.M.	Reading Classified Ads. Only two listed in my field.	Hopeless Helpless (Worthless)	They won't hire an unemployed loser like me.	Many applying will not have the degree I hold. That's a plus for me.	A little better
10 A.M.	Argument with ten-year-old son over his messy room.	(Hopeless) (Helpless) Worthless	I can't control this kid.	He's become less compliant due to stress in the house. Could be a lot worse (truancy, lying, poor grades).	A lot better
3 P.M.	Lying on couch thinking about all the bills.	(Hopeless) Helpless Worthless	I'll never get out from under this debt.	We've always been able to get out of bad patches together. This depression makes everything seem impossible.	A little better
8 P.M.	Called two friends. Neither one was home.	Hopeless Helpless (Worthless)	I have nobody, and it's because I'm just a total nothing to be with.	My wife loves me, kids, sister. It's 8 P.M. on Friday. Many people have made plans and are out by 8.	A lot better

Methods of Thought Debate

1. *Bring exceptions into awareness.* Depressed people tend to think in all-or-nothing terms. Challenge your automatic thought with at least one valid exception. Let's look at an example. *Thought:* "My kids are having problems; therefore I'm a bad mother." *Argument:* "I've made sacrifices so that I'm home when they get home from school. I haven't ignored the problems; rather I'm trying to nip them in the bud. I've never been abusive to my kids, I've told them I love them regularly and I've always provided for them."

2. *Bring in external data.* Depressed people blame bad things solely on internal qualities. Bring information about the situation that is outside of you into the argument. *Thought:* "My depression is the sole cause of my marital problems." *Argument:* Financial problems have worsened of late; my husband is out of work and this has contributed to our problems; our kids have gone away to college, forcing us to focus on existing problems; and my husband has not tried to understand the depression I'm in."

3. *The Dr. Frankenstein Technique:* Remember, here you create someone else from scratch who would fit the bill 100%. For example, if you recently broke up and now think you are unlovable, you can create a "monster" that is undisputedly 100% unlovable. Then using information about yourself that is different from the "monster" you've created, argue your case. *Thought:* "I'm unlovable." *Argument:* "A monster that is totally unlovable would be completely selfish and without the capacity for giving. I have friends who have told me I'm worthwhile. Plus, I attract people. My problem is that I get too clingy and demanding once I'm in a relationship. That's different from being unlovable."

4. *Get rid of global generalizations.* Depressed people tend to make attributions of global disaster. Argue the thought by making it more specific. *Thought:* "All my

relationships are messed up." *Argument:* "I haven't had problems with my close friends; in fact, they've grown closer since my marital problems. My problems are specifically in the romantic area, an area where trust is a particular issue."

5. *Argue that it ain't gonna last.* Depressed people think the bad is never going to end, that the negative will endure until the end of time. Make an argument that current problems are temporary by thinking about times when bad patches have been overcome and think about aspects of the situation that are not permanent (or don't have to be permanent). *Thought:* "I'll never be able to work again." *Argument:* "I've worked all my life until lately, when work stress and relationship stress got so overwhelming that I fell into depression. The depression made it impossible to work. I didn't know how to get out of it. But now, I'm getting treatment for the depression. Once the depression has lifted, I'll be able to get back to my productive life."

6. *Compare to others who are worse off.* Depressed people tend to compare themselves only to people who are functioning better than they are. It can literally seem like everybody is better off. Bring into your argument folks and situations that are worse off than you are. Sounds insensitive, but compared to the depressive comparisons, it can really put things into balance. *Thought:* "I've messed up worse than anyone by getting fired from a job." *Argument:* "Not true; my brother has never been able to hold a job for more than a month, but I've held jobs as long as five years, until lately due to stress with my kids. My niece has never worked at all. Now she's in for some grim surprises once she needs to work!"

7. *The debate assignment.* Imagine you and someone else have experienced the exact same life situations. Your "twin" has been assigned the task of defending the thought you've identified, and you have been assigned

the task of refuting it. How would you succeed? (Hint: it might have something to do with countering ideas of complete hopelessness, absolute worthlessness, and total helplessness, or all three). This technique, though artificial, gets you thinking from other vantage points. Sometimes going through the motions puts you in a frame of mind such that you can really consider them as valid. For example, if the *thought* is "I'm an idiot," you might imagine your twin listing evidence to the fact, like "You lost your job, you can't pay all your bills, and your son is doing poorly in school." Then offer your *argument* by imagining the opposing comebacks a good debater would make, such as "People lose jobs for many reasons other than being an idiot; a lot of stress can influence one's performance at work. I was certainly smart enough to land the job. Once these stressors are overcome, I'll be able to work again, and also be able to catch up on the bills." Your twin might come back with, "Yeah, but only an idiot would let stress take over his life," to which you might come back (again imagining yourself as being adept at arguing a position) by replying that "An idiot would have been taken down by every little crisis that came up. I've made it through lots of problems in the past. Every man has his limit, and mine was reached. An idiot might just wallow in it, but I'm putting effort into solving these problems and getting back on my feet." You'll find that as your twin continues to try backing up such negative generalizations as "idiot," his reasoning will seem more and more flawed.

More Metacognitive Hammers

In addition to the pencil and paper exercises presented so far, you need to start doing metacognitive work in your head. Some patients in the outpatient cognitive therapy program felt that the paper and pencil exercises were tedious

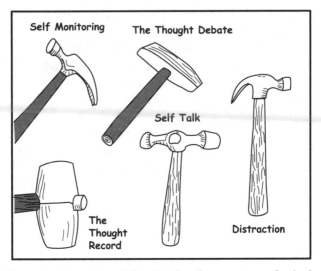

Self Monitoring   The Thought Debate

Self Talk

The Thought Record   Distraction

Important tools to add to the hardware store of mind.

and believed that they could do the exercises mentally. I've found that the greatest benefit from cognitive therapy comes from doing both; that is, regularly completing thought records as well as tangling with negative thoughts in your head.

The Cognitive Thermometer

When you're sick, you take your temperature to see if you have a fever. When you're depressed, you need to gauge another temperature: your cognitive temperature. I've stressed from the get-go that increasing your self-awareness by self-monitoring is going to help you develop cognitive skills faster. But what I've found is that patients either forget to self-monitor, only do it when prompted by someone (usually the therapist), or they don't do it enough.

We get so used to the negative mindset of depression that we sort of become numb to it. Anything that increases our ability to catch and distract from or dispute these thoughts lessens depression's ability to keep a foothold. Unfortunately, there's no product on the market for taking your cognitive temperature, but, thankfully, we have metacognition, which does the job just fine.

Think of things that might serve as reminders to check your thinking. For people who refer to a calendar or organizer regularly, a "code" penciled in at several points in the day can be helpful. Some watches and pagers have alarm features. Anything that can serve as a reminder is appropriate. Paul Gilbert, in *Overcoming Depression: A Step-by-Step Approach to Gaining Control over Depression* (1997), recommends that people carry some sort of object in their pockets, like a stone or a ring. Every those people jam their hand in their pocket, they can assess their thinking.

If I need to remember something, I usually write it on my hand. "Cog Temp" or "Triad" or "Ogre" written on your palm can help you check into what's brewing in your skull more often (although friends and nosey people may ask you what the hand note is for). You'll be surprised how many times you actually look at your hands. Those small round colored labels are good too. Stick them here and there, especially places you look at often.

You want to install into your day regular reminders to kick start metacognition and assess thoughts of self, control, and future. In terms of self, ask yourself, "How am I stacking up right now? How would I rate myself?" Then move to control and ask, "How powerful am I today? Do I have control over important areas?" Then do the same with future, asking, "How's my tomorrow shaping up? Is there some light at the end of the tunnel? Are there things to look forward to?" If you notice anything foul and ugly in your thinking, dispute it; argue with it. The goal is to keep your "reality" as far from hopeless, helpless, and worthless and as close to hopeful, powerful, and worthy as possible.

Cue Words

Cue words are often used to help people with anger control problems (e.g., Feindler, 1990). In the outpatient cognitive therapy program, we help angry patients associate the physical symptoms that tend to occur early on in an angry escalation with a word that alerts them to a potential problem, and the need to initiate coping strategies. A fellow named Michael, who had a nasty hostility problem, noticed that his leg would shake as the early agitation of angry arousal set in. In cognitive behavior therapy, he began to practice saying, "Anger alert" to himself each time he noticed his leg shaking, which reminded him that his anger tended have a rapid onset with awful consequences, and that he needed to cool down now. In time, with repeated pairing of the cue word with the physiological arousal, the cue word would come to mind automatically each time his leg would twitch and shake. With practice, Michael had instilled a reliable anger alarm.

You can develop cue words yourself associated with any of the depressive symptoms presented. Periods of deep sorrow are common with depression and sometimes seem to just come out of nowhere. Assign a cue word to these experiences. When you notice tearfulness coming on, say loudly to yourself, "Cognitive time!" or "Thought debate!" or "Ogre thrashing!" or simply, "Stop!" With repeated pairing and subsequent argument with the thoughts, it will become more natural, and Big Bad Thoughts won't slip through as easily.

Question Thyself

The easiest method of increasing patches of relief is to ask yourself questions. Not just any question, like "Why does ketchup come in a bottle while mustard comes in a jar?" but the right questions. Below are the type of questions you want to start posing when depression rears its ugly head.

• **What would "Coping Joe" or "Coping Jill" (someone I admire greatly and who copes well) say to themselves in this situation?**

We all know some "Coping Joe" or some "Coping Jill." That's the guy or gal who seems to always have a realistic, healthy, accurate conceptualization of things—even when they're having a difficult time! Ask yourself what this coping person might be thinking if the same thing was happening to him or her. If you've just suffered a break up with your boyfriend, ask yourself, "What would Coping Susan, who has a strong positive self concept, say to herself if she was in my same situation?" Sometimes assigning the negative event to someone we admire and imagining how he or she would cope with it is helpful. First, we are put in a position to consider that it is possible to view the situation differently; second, once we think about the coping strategies another person might use, we can see those strategies as something we could use, too.

• **What would I say to "Vulnerable Vic" or "Vulnerable Vanessa" (my son, daughter, lover, best friend, or someone else I care deeply for) if they were voicing this thought?**

Here, you want to imagine either someone you care deeply about, such as your son or daughter or spouse, or someone to whom you provide guidance and care because they're on the vulnerable side. This disputation question takes advantage of the fact that we are all better therapists to others than we are to ourselves. Usually we have many good responses and a knapsack of good advice for their problems and negative generalizations. The problem is that we don't see that advice as applicable to ourselves. Mentally put yourself in a position of "therapizing" someone you care about. What would you say if she was in your boat? It is absolutely amazing how much common sense, compassion, and rational thinking will flow out when you plant the awful thought on someone else. The trick, however, is to then ask yourself if any of the advice you gave to "Vulnerable Vera" applies to you.

• **If I were less depressed about this situation, what would I be thinking?**

This is a wonderful cognitive strategy I've used many times in cognitive groups. A patient will come in swilled to the gills in gloom, lamenting all her defeats, and I'll ask her if she could imagine someone experiencing the same life events but not being as depressed about them. At first the patient usually disagrees, but after discussion and feedback from others as to the effect of our appraisals on how we feel, she will usually admit that all events, from marital troubles to job stress or whatever, can have a variety of emotional consequences depending on how we think about it. Asking the patient to conjure up the thoughts a non-depressed person might be having is a powerful process.

Beth recently experienced a divorce, and was quite depressed. When she noticed the presence of self blaming and hopeless thoughts, she found it useful to imagine what her friend Gloria, who had had a divorce and had managed well, might be thinking. Such thoughts included, "I've learned from this experience. I need to stop falling for these types of guys. I can do it." Putting positive thoughts in your head may sound a little like relying just on positive thinking, but it's different. The thoughts of a non-depressed person are not unanimously positive. Some are positive, some are sort of positive, most are neutral, and some are negative. With this form of disputation, you are putting realistic, rational thoughts in your head, and then attempting to make a case that there is some truth to them.

• What from my past argues that this thought is not true?

This question is good for almost all black and white negative thoughts, but is particularly good for hopeless thoughts. "I'll never get over this" all by itself is as grim as it gets. If you can pull up memories of negative experiences you've been able to overcome, you can use those memories to challenge the certainty of hopeless predictions. Try to remember as many as possible. The more the better, in terms of struggles defeated, as it is common for depressed people to uphold the idea that "this is different." If you can remember a variety of bad patches you've been able to get past, you can counter the thought that "this is different" with "they all were different."

Coping Cards

At the end of this book, there are five *Coping Cards* designed to help you become more able to argue with yourself in the heat of the moment. There is a coping card for depression, one for suicidal thoughts, one for anxiety, one for motivation, and another for anger. Simply remove them from the book and keep them in places where you'll see them regularly, such as in your purse, wallet, or car, or in the kitchen, by the phone, or on the nightstand. If the time is not right to do a thought record, whip out one of the coping cards. Review the disputation questions and ponder them. Patients have reported that the coping cards have really helped to remind them of the cognitive therapy tools throughout the day.

Dispelling Depressive Attributions

Since the late 1970s, Lyn Abramson, Martin Seligman and their colleagues have been interested in how depressed people's conclusions about negative and positive life events differed from the conclusions of non-depressed people (e.g., Abramson, Seligman, & Teasdale, 1978; Seligman, Abramson, Semmel, & von Baeyer, 1979). Their early research served as a foundation for much of what cognitive therapy addresses today. These researchers and their colleagues discovered that, as opposed to non-depressed people, depressed people tend to make internal, global, stable attributions about negative events, and to make external, specific and unstable attributions about positive events. Putting it another way, depressed people tend to think that negative events come from within themselves, apply to everything, and are unchangeable. Depressed people tend to think that positive events come from outside themselves, are caused by a definite reason, and can be changed.

For example, imagine a depressed man and non-depressed man each receiving a negative critique from his boss. When something negative like this happens, the depressed man is more likely to come to the conclusion that it was due to something about himself that is overriding and not likely to change. "I'm stupid" would be an example of an internal, global, stable attribution. Stupidity is an internal quality of the host, it is global (stupidity tends to be all consuming) and it's stable (people don't usually outgrow stupidity; once you got it, it's there for good).

Now, if the boss offered a positive critique, the depressed man would be more likely than the non-depressed man to conclude that it was due to external, specific and unstable factors. Such a conclusion might be, "My boss is just feeling sorry for me lately." Here, the reason for the positive critique is not due to talent or dedication, which would be an internal, global, and stable attribution, but rather a quality of the boss that may very well be transient.

In other words, depressed people truly rip themselves off. Bad things happen? "I caused it. I'll continue to cause it." Good things happen? "It was the other guy, or just luck."

Given these results, it would follow that a great way to apply metacognition would be to try to reverse this tendency; that is, when a good thing happens, fight the depressive knee jerk reaction and attempt to consider internal, global and stable factors that led to its occurrence. For bad events, do just the opposite, and instead of coming to internal, global and stable attributions, consider factors outside yourself. Look for evidence that the bad event is specific to a narrow range of experience, that it's not permanent.

It would be a bit of denial to make external, specific, and unstable attributions to all negative events, as would viewing every good thing that happened as due to some internal, global, and stable quality. But you may be able to alter one or two distorted components of an attribution. For example, let's say a friend calls out of the blue and offers support. After your friend's visit, you come to the conclusion that "My friends just feel sorry for me." This would be an external, specific, unstable attribution. However, let's say that, after you consider the history of the relationship, you change the attribution to "My friends really care about me." This would be an external, global, stable attribution. Or let's

Bad Event	**Good Event**
Consider:	*Consider:*
• Causes outside of me	• Internal qualities contributing to the event's occurrence.
• Consider the bad event as a single episode, due to specific determinant, not some global, all-consuming cause.	• That these qualities are not just specific to this situation, but play out in other areas too.
• Consider the event as temporary, and you as not necessarily doomed to future replays of this event.	• That the good event is not a fluke. It can happen again.

say you snapped at your child, and came to the conclusion, "I'm a terrible mother," which is an internal, global, stable attribution. However, after considering the fact that you've been struggling with depression, and remembering that before you were depressed you rarely snapped at your children, you are able to change the attribution to "My depression has influenced my patience with my kids," you have come up with an internal, specific, unstable attribution.

Talking Back to Suicidal Thoughts

Suicidal thinking is serious. Not all depressed people have suicidal thoughts, but some do, and the times when someone is thinking about suicide would be the most vital times to apply cognitive strategies. Metacognition has definitely saved lives. People who were experiencing thoughts about dying have managed to "talk themselves out of it" and changed their minds. Depressed people have reported being pushed to the edge by some last-straw negative event and having vivid urges of self-doom, but electing not to act on them because of some steadfast value that forbids the act.

Remember, cognitive techniques are not foolproof. Thoughts about suicide should not be kept secret. If you find yourself unable to make the thoughts go away, it is vital that you talk to someone who takes you seriously and can assure your safety.

Below are some arguments that can be effective in making suicidal thoughts go away.

1. *Suicidal thinking is caused by depression, not life events.* If you go searching for a suicidal person that is feeling good, you're gonna have a long journey ahead of you. People with psychotic delusions aside, non-depressed people don't consider suicide, even when their lives are riddled with defeat. Countless times I've listened to people who were hospitalized for severe depression speak of the absolute hopelessness of their situation, then, several weeks later, when the depression has begun to lift, rescind these ideas. And, get this, many have experienced very little—if any—actual life change! In other words, they've left the hospital to the same life events that seemed to "rationalize" suicide as an option, but were no longer contemplating the act because the depression has lifted. Depression clogs the holes of happy future. It makes everything good seem impossible to attain; every prognosis, hopeless. You need to remind yourself that suicidal thoughts ride on depression, and they couldn't even saddle up otherwise. The depression is what needs to be eliminated.

2. *Suicidal thoughts are temporary. They go away.* Most depressed folks who have thought about suicide have thought about it before. It has always eventually disappeared, and when it did, all things seemed different, even when there hadn't been that much actual change in the environment. For people thinking about suicide, it can be a lifesaver if they remind themselves of that fact. Perhaps they remember a time when the kind word of another person helped them regain their faith in people's loyalty or gave them hope that relationships can improve, or times when they've received helpful

information about the things that were upsetting them (like news from a creditor that spreading out payments is okay). If you're having thoughts of self harm, think about the times thoughts like this have gone away, and why. It can be helpful to remember that if thoughts of suicide were true, they couldn't come and go.

3. *"Hey, I wasn't suicidal an hour ago (or a day ago)."* Ask yourself, "Have things really changed that much since I wasn't suicidal to justify this irreversible act?" Usually some stressful event pushes a person to considering suicide.

I recall a fellow called Dan who was morbidly depressed after he got a divorce and became estranged from his son. Months had gone by, and Dan had become more and more depressed, but not suicidal. Then his wedding anniversary popped up on the calendar, and suddenly, Dan was talking suicide. I recall asking him, "Hey, Dan, yesterday you were talking about returning to work; what was that all about?"

Dan said, "It's all over. That was nonsense."

But I'm not gonna let Dan off that easy, so I said, "No, wait; I was sitting right here, and you said, 'I'm feeling like it would be good for me to go back to work.' Then you said, 'Maybe things could get better.' You even agreed with some suggestions from others in group that it might be nice for you to start hitting the gym again with your pals."

Dan considered this for several moments, then he snapped back into depression mode, saying, "Yeah, I said that yesterday. I was full of nonsense yesterday. Today I have more clarity."

So I said, "Listen, Dan, I hear you juggling balls of logic here, but let me ask you, yesterday did all that stuff you said feel true?"

Dan, after pondering for a spell, said, "It did."

So, I asked him why, and Dan said, "Because I felt much better."

Keeping with the swing, I said, "Dan, all we have since yesterday is a spin of the clock. Nothing else has really happened. Tell me, Dan, if you'd not known today was your anniversary, if you'd forgotten all about it, what might you be thinking and feeling now?

He answered, "Probably the same as yesterday. You're right. I'm doing this to myself by thinking more about my divorce today. Nothing has happened that undoes what I said yesterday."

Why did Dan feel better after this bit of Socratic litigation? Because he realized that what was really making him feel bad was his dredging up of memories. He realized that he had not felt suicidal a day before and that nothing had really changed since then to justify the idea of taking his life.

Stupid Ogres

In Chapter One, I offered Richard's likening of depression to a filthy ogre sitting on his chest. One thing I like about his analogy is that ogres aren't very smart. Neither is depression. It's just a nasty bully. This chapter is chock-full of tricks. Yes, tricks. The idea of tricking the depression can also provide an extra push, especially if you're the sort who doesn't like to be outsmarted.

Every time you are able to diminish depression, even for just a little while, you are tricking the depression. If you complete the Thought Record Flow Sheet exercise, or the Thought Debate, and consequently enjoy a two-hour patch of improved mood, you've essentially won an intellectual battle with the ogre. Yeah, I know, the ogre keeps coming back, like some stupid schoolyard thug. But remember, these thugs are always eventually pressed down. It's always brain over brawn in the long run.

Main Points

1. The thought record's just one way to flex your meta-cognitive muscle. There's also a bunch of other ways that are quicker. Some are simpler pencil and paper exercises, plus, there are dozens of tricks you can prac-

tice doing in your head.

2. The Thought Debate, like the Thought Record, is a pencil and paper exercise which helps you develop a convincing argument and apply it to Big Bad Thoughts. People who benefit from the Thought Debate do at least five of them per day.

3. The ultimate goal of cognitive therapy is for people to be able to monitor thinking regularly, catch cognitive errors, and correct them quickly and efficiently. It helps to use reminders to check into your automatic thinking throughout the day. Using stickers or other props can increase your self-awareness. The repeated pairing of a cue word to the rising physical symptoms of depression will train you to clue into fluctuations in mood and not miss the opportunity to take control.

4. Asking yourself questions is a good way to discover sneaky negative thinking and to challenge it. The right questions can help you view an arbitrary conclusion from another's vantage point, a vantage point you might take if the situation was modified, and from vantage points more accurately tied to the facts.

5. Talking yourself out of suicide is a skill you must master to total reliability. You can successfully reduce those suicidal thoughts by reminding yourself that it is depression, not life events, that causes suicidal thinking. It can be helpful to remember that suicidal thoughts are temporary and always go away. Ask yourself what has really changed from the time you were not suicidal to now, when you are having thoughts of suicide. Often, in the grand scheme, not much has occurred; rather, some event has felt like the last straw. However, that last straw is not reason in and of itself to die. Further, remembering the reasons for living that you had before you thought about suicide—which is often just hours ago—and asking if their truth has really changed since then can dampen suicidal thoughts. Using metacognition to counter suicidal

thoughts is an important skill, but is no substitute for getting help from caring people. A supportive person is in a much better state of mind to talk you out of suicidal ideas and plans and to get you to a safe place if the ideas refuse to vanish.

Chapter Six:

Social Skills 101

Let's face it, when we're depressed, we're often no picnic to spend time with. Depression can make us morose, preoccupied, irritable, disinterested, and tired. Plus, we usually don't look as nice as we used to. For some folks, gray sweats and slippers are over represented. Combs seem to have lost their teeth or something, and it's like benching two-twenty to upside-down that frown.

You often read in the popular press that people shouldn't "put on a happy face" for others if they aren't, in fact, happy; that this is "inauthentic" or even "codependent" behavior. However, smiling and appearing happy can be quite helpful when you're depressed. All the time? Certainly not. Occasionally for the purpose of enhancing a social encounter? Yes, definitely.

Earlier, social isolation was presented as a "classic" depressive symptom. Depressed people often cocoon themselves in their homes or apartments. Socialization feels like it's going to be unrewarding and laborious. But listen, you want to know a grim fact? Not only do depressed people pull away from others, but people tend to pull away from depressed people too.

Guest Repellent

Why would someone decrease time spent with a suffering friend or loved one? It could be looked at as a pretty selfish thing to do to someone suffering from something as horrible as depression. This may be so in some circumstances, from "friends" or associates who, when the tables turn and they're expected to give a little, do an about face and disappear. But this isn't always the case.

There are many reasons why even real friends might keep a distance from a depressed person. First, they may not

**A depressed person can literally
go through cans of the stuff.**

understand depression and may come to some other conclusion about the depressed person's radical change in
behavior and appearance. The distance some depressed
people put between themselves and others may convey
incorrectly that they're not as interested in their friendship
any more. Remember, with only vague clues, people are left
to their own interpretations.

Or, people may feel that they are causing more harm than
good. My friend may be thinking, "I've tried everything to
help Bob, but he just keeps getting worse. Maybe he needs
some distance from me. I'm clearly not helping. Maybe this
thing needs to run its course." Still another reason may be
that the depression seems contagious. Let's face it; depression is depressing.

Moreover, if someone has actually suffered a bout of depression in the past, spending time with a depressed person can be quite scary. Vivid and emotionally tainted memories can become activated, and people may want to simply protect themselves from relapse (not that a relapse would necessarily occur, but flashbacks of a clinical depression are absolutely dreadful).

The focus right now is not to make you feel guilty for pushing people away, but to work on ways to improve your socialization. It can be very hard to believe it when we're depressed, but that's when we need people more than ever. People can be medicinal. Not all people, of course; there are a few at the low end of my New Year's Eve party invitation list who'd be about as medicinal if I were depressed as watching a sad and dreary movie while sitting alone in the dark on a Saturday night.

But certain people really can pull us out of the dark for a bit. And we want to access these people and take advantage of their potential for offering us a patch of relief. For a friend to call and remind you that he or she still cares can have a tremendous effect on depression. Maybe it's not a lasting effect, but remember, kicking depression's ugly butt is about increasing the patches of relief. Increasing the frequency of positive social encounters is one way of doing this.

You may be thinking that you don't need to read a discussion on social skills. You may have a history of very effective socialization. Here's what I've seen: even folks who were at the pinnacle of fashion and boasting top grades in social skillery can land a grade of "D-" when depression starts raining blackly. Emphasis on social skill enhancement is appropriate for almost everyone who is struggling with depression. You may be having only minor social skill deficits, like problems with eye contact, or problems smiling, but the little nuances in our social interactions are just as important as the really obvious ones in terms of smooth-running relationships.

Defining Social Skill

What are "social skills" anyway? If they're "skills," then people must vary in terms of how many they possess and how good they are at them. This is very true. A social skill is a behavior that encourages others to want to have a relationship with you. And remember, there's a pretty broad spectrum of contacts that could be termed "relationship." Relationships range from the brief exchange with the clerk who's ringing up your bag of party ice to a thirty-year marriage.

All relationships require skills. We all need to possess something, some bait, which we can cast into the people pool out there, to hook and reel in a catch. If I lack social skills, all those people will just swim by and dart toward the fishermen and fisherwomen who have the right bait. And people are very finicky when it comes to social skill bait. You may think you have the appropriate social skills for a certain pool, but if

Social fishing: It's all about the right bait.

they're even slightly the wrong flavor, the people you want to attract will zip away from you like you're a cheap lure.

"I Don't Care What Other People Think of Me!"

When we're depressed, we tell ourselves that we'd be better off by ourselves. The company of others doesn't seem that appealing, so we isolate ourselves. Remember, this is a symptom of depression, and is one of the symptoms that can prolong depression.

Depression is an alienating experience. Depression makes us dig a lonely sand hole and languish in its shadowy bottom without a soul to communicate with. Recognizing that you can connect with people, respond to questions, partake in conversations, and earn a compliment reminds you that you're still human.

Social Skill Basics

Research supports *social skills training* for depressed individuals as a powerful method for reducing depression (e.g., Bellack, Hersen, & Himmelhoch, 1983). There are whole volumes written that focus on the enhancement of depressed people's social skills. As we discussed earlier, even mild depression can influence your social skills, and a decline in social skills may not be helping you conquer the depression. The importance of addressing the tangible symptoms of depression has already been emphasized. Social skill deficits are definitely tangible. Let's look at each of three social skill areas typically influenced by depression: hygiene and attire, body language, and verbal communication.

Hygiene and Attire

How you look, smell, sound, and taste matters. Now it may seem infantalizing to go over something as preschool as tending to bathing, shaving, and shoe-dress-blouse combinations; but like me with the piano, go a month or two without practice, and you can get pretty rusty. Not everyone who suffers from depression neglects "activities of daily living." But many do. The discussion below offers a good opportunity to think about how you tend to your hygiene and appearance now, compared to how you tended to those tasks before you were depressed.

First, you need to shower or bathe regularly. Shampoo regularly, too. Not only does it get you moving and make you feel better, you really do look better. That brings us to hairstyle. Style your hair as you did before you were depressed. If you've not done anything with it for a couple months, then a hair cut or styling is probably a good idea. I've encouraged very depressed people to get a haircut and invariably their mood has perked the next day. That improvement is without a doubt due to the people around them who said they noticed and liked the change, and the realization that they really could make themselves better. By the way, a "no bed head" rule can make it difficult to languish in bed or on the couch during the day, because of the effort it will take to restyle the hair after it's been slept on.

The sense of smell is powerful and mysterious. There are times when I smell something and my mood starts leaping and flailing spastic—and I can't always put my finger on why! Take advantage of olfactory allure. Ladies, if you're in a depression, that's the time to dig your colognes, perfumes and powders out of the back of the cabinet or visit one of those soapy bath stores in the mall. For women who wear makeup and fragrances, there's nothing like a new shade of lipstick or a new scent of perfume to give you a boost of confidence.

And guys, even though you might be currently out of work because of this horrible depressive patch, you need to shave regularly. Shaving daily keeps you in a functional mode. Even though you are not feeling functional, you don't want to look like you've thrown in the towel. Of course this doesn't apply to gentlemen who have a well-maintained mustache and/or beard. I'm not suggesting you need to have a shorn face to look good. However, your face should be groomed daily.

Brushing and flossing every day is about as basic as it gets, but when you're depressed, even this daily routine can seem futile and tedious. Depression is often heaviest in the morning, so take advantage of anything that might energize you. Every little bit counts when we're talking about motivating ourselves to get up and moving. The exhilaration of a brushing, flossing and gargling with mouthwash can have the same effect as a cold shower. And a little energy can make a big difference when we're talking about getting moving in the morning.

Clothes are an awesome lure for compliments, smiles, and double takes. The basics: clothing should be clean, pressed, coordinated, and appropriate for the situation, just like it was before the depression hit.

Think about treating yourself to a new article of clothing. You may not think you deserve one because productivity has suffered in so many areas, but no one is more deserving of a new shirt than a person in the mire of depression.

This is not meant to sound insensitive to people who are on a slender budget. I'm not suggesting that people need to go out and purchase a new spring wardrobe to get out of depression. I've encountered many depressed folks who are having financial problems, and consequently have fewer garments to choose from, but nonetheless have a mountain of laundry waiting in front of the washer. Clean up what you have, work within your budget, and think about coordinating outfits like it mattered.

Also, with regard to the wardrobe, the attractive stuff tends to be underrepresented when we're depressed. It's like we don't feel worthy of our favorite slacks. What gets worn is the easy stuff, the outfits you can literally pour yourself into, like frayed sweats, faded T-shirts, holey pairs of jeans, slippers, and flip-flops.

It's always so encouraging to see depressed patients begin to dress in a way that shows that they put time into it.

It is usually a sign that they are starting to feel better. I recall a patient who came to the first group cognitive therapy session in pajamas. Then, she graduated to sweats. In time, as the depression lifted, she was wearing jeans and T-shirts. On her last day of the program she looked absolutely lovely in a very put together outfit. She said, "I wore this to my last job interview. I don't have a job interview today, but I just felt like wearing it."

Body Language

Nonverbal communication is powerful; it can be a much more powerful communicator than what you actually say. It can enhance what you say; it can contradict what you say. This aspect of social skills is a bit harder to address, as most of our body language is habitual and is sometimes very ingrained. Every part of your body has the potential to convey something, though it may not be what you want to convey. For example, I have this tendency to shake my leg when I'm restless. Sometimes I don't want people to know I'm restless. My leg doesn't really care about what I want, however. It shakes when it wants to. Changes in body language due to depression are similarly involuntary. It's like all of the natural fluctuations in body tone, facial muscle and eye movements have lost connection to their power source. This affects relationships because people use their partners' body language to gauge how they're doing. If the expected movements or reactions (such as a nod of agreement or widening of eyes in response to a surprising anecdote) don't occur, some people might get uncomfortable, or jump to conclusions based on their own doubts and insecurities. This is especially true for people who do not know you are suffering from depression.

Depressed people often lug themselves around like a sack of dirty laundry, which might convey to others that they are not a good investment of interactive energy. Though it is hard, attempt to stand and sit in a way that doesn't make it look like you haven't slept in a decade.

Regarding the face: in terms of socialization, this is the most opportunity-dense part of the anatomy. For a relatively small round patch of sensory knobs, intake holes and hair, it's truly amazing how much can be conveyed to other round patches of sensory knobs, intake holes and hair without even speaking.

Eyes convey so much: love, interest, joy, happiness, astonishment, to name a few. However, eye contact seems very difficult if we are depressed. We feel so rotten about ourselves that we think others are viewing us the same way. So we look at the floor, making it impossible for anyone else to catch any of the emotions in our eyes. To counter this, try to increase eye contact when you are interacting with other people, despite the pull to look away. It's uncomfortable to increase eye contact when you've been looking at the floor for a while, so start with small amounts. Work your way up from five-second patches of eye contact with the clerk in the discount store to ten-second patches, and so forth. Like most anxiety-provoking behavioral changes, this typically gets easier with practice.

The mouth too has a fully functional language without words. Even when you're not talking, your mouth should move sometimes. Smiling is one of the most difficult things to do when you're depressed. Some people think it's tantamount to "being inauthentic" and wonder why they should smile when they feel like crying. As I said, "being inauthentic" by not giving into depression's desire to send you to bed for whole afternoons is not the same as "being inauthentic" in order to please others or to avoid conflict. You're "being inauthentic" to trick the depression. When the depression has broken, the action will feel more natural.

The face muscles need to flex and unflex with the changing tone of our interactions. If you've been depressed for a while, you may think you've forgotten how to move your face. The natural facial flex will return when you are feeling better. For now, you are going to have to remind yourself to move your face. Take a walk some place where people are chatting, and hone in on their faces. "Man, look at those cheeks, those eyeball sockets, that forehead, that nose, and those lips," you might think. Faces get strenuous workouts even when someone's just listening.

One way of demonstrating to yourself that these mannerisms are still in your brain is to look in the mirror and try to activate certain moods. Try "anger" first. Watch your eyebrows cave in and your upper lip climb your face like someone snagged it with a fishing hook. Next, do "excitement." Watch your eye sockets yawn as your whole face stretches. Now do "amused." See how your eyes get squinty?

Some people have a more agitated depression and consequently have developed fidgety habits, such as biting their nails or tapping on things. Some will wring their hands like washcloths or chew the inside of their mouths. These habits can be distracting and interfere with smooth relating. If you have such habits, you can alter them by training yourself to clue into them when they occur. The use of cue words was discussed earlier with regard to anger and alerting yourself to depressive dips. You can teach your brain to be quickly aware of something like lip biting by reciting a cue word whenever you notice it occurring or feel the urge to do so. Think "No bite!" or even pinch yourself on your arm or thigh when you notice the habit occurring. Frequent interruption of a nervous habit decreases its strength.

Verbal Communication

The most sophisticated of all social skills is the ability to initiate and swing with conversation. Our ability to talk to others is influenced by depression mostly because of the impairments to concentration, memory retrieval and attention. Discussion requires conscious effortful thinking, retrieval of information, attention to incoming information and the ability to move with transitions. Depression slows things down. It's like someone dumped a half-gallon of pan-cake syrup into the cog wheels of our thinking apparatus. Our verbal communication becomes infrequent, slowed, awkward, off base, and often can't achieve the levels of abstract conceptualization we used to reach.

Let's start with tone of conversation. Depressed people can come across as very negative and overly self-focused. Remember, it's natural when we're depressed to be nega-tively self-absorbed, and therefore, it becomes "natural" to talk about negative, self-focused topics when others are present.

Most informal conversations don't hold up well when the tone is overly negative. Remember, due to the miserable downward stream of consciousness that occurs when we're depressed, any topic can be twisted into something ugly. I've witnessed depressed people morph a completely pleas-ant discussion into something morbid. Conversations can go like this: "Gee, Phil, when I approached you, we were talking about the kids' soccer game and how well they're doing, and now we're talking about how polluted the beaches are. How'd that happen?"

Monitor the "topic mood" of your interactions with peo-ple. If the tone starts positive, try to maintain it, not pull it down into the bog. Also, diminish what is referred to as "chronic symptom recital." Depressed people feel the need to talk about their depressive symptoms a lot, just like some people with chronic pain talk about their physical discom-fort incessantly. For the pain patient, not only does this make the pain seem worse by the inordinate attention paid to it, but also it drains relationships. This should not be interpreted as "never talk about your depression." Cer-tainly, getting support from people is vital when you are depressed, and especially if you are having hopeless thoughts or thoughts of self harm. But depression doesn't need to be the number one topic of every single conversa-tion. It can become exhausting for you and for your friends and intimates.

Sometimes when I've encouraged depressed patients to make more verbal contact with people, they think I'm asking them to tell more people about their depression. This is not the case. Depressed people need to work on balancing the topics of conversation. For example, your friend may want to spend some time discussing the depression because she's concerned about it, but this doesn't mean the whole evening needs to be spent talking about it. You may end up feeling more gloomy, or guilty even, after so much self-focus. Or you might feel relieved, but your friend may leave feeling completely drained.

There should be a relative balance in the me-you focus. Depressed people will sometimes walk away from a conversation not knowing a thing about the person they've just talked with for half an hour. Sometimes it's because of the concentration problems of depression but it can also be due to the fact that the depressed person's partner never got a chance to elaborate on anything because the conversation was constantly bent back toward the depressed person and his or her problems.

One way to balance a conversation is to ask questions. If you find yourself talking a lot, pause and ask for feedback. Ask the person you are talking with if she has something in common from her experience. Or use a question to change the subject. Practice following up on what the other person has said, and asking questions to get more information about that person.

Initiation is a crucial social skill. Depressed people will often put themselves in situations where there are people, but then just stand there waiting for someone to strike up conversation. Often they come home feeling more alienated and invisible than they did before they went. If it's been a while since you've struck up many conversations, start in situations where there is little risk, such as with family and friends, or low risk public settings, like in the grocery or the bookstore.

Maintaining appropriate voice volume and gauging rate of speech are also important social skills. Depressed people tend to speak in a flat monotone, and to speak too slowly. This makes sense, as lively discussion usually has enthusiasm to drive it, and enthusiasm is something depressed people are usually lacking. Try to mirror the volume and intonations of people with whom you are interacting.

**Because of depression's effect on facial expression
and tone of voice, it would be hard to know
from this exchange that Brenda actually likes
Dan's new Bird-with-Worm tattoo a lot.**

You may think that you will not have the energy to reach the vocal levels of non-depressed people, and this may be true, but a little may go a long way in terms of adding some color to a monotonous conversational style.

Another thing that can happen when you're depressed, again mostly due to the information processing deficits and biases, is that you drift in and out of the conversation. This is a process that is very difficult to alter, as it feels like there is a current in your depressed head pulling your consciousness to drift. Work on really focusing on what is being discussed. Some depressed people will contribute to a conversation with reflections of what has been said to them. When listening to someone speak, try to remark intermittently. This can be a good way to keep on track and show others that you are listening, and most importantly, to help you avoid negative self-focused material.

If you've found yourself tuning out, and are asked a question, instead of guessing whether or not the topic has changed, ask a question back to get back on track. If the conversation is a mile and a half away from where it was when you detoured into self-absorption, saying something like, "I'm not sure I understood completely your last remark; can you explain it?" or "I'm intrigued; tell me more," may give you enough clues that you can unmoor yourself and get back into the flow.

Improving social skills will be easier for some people than others, and the tips offered here may simply not be enough for some others. It's been said many times before, but when depression is so heavy that you can't change some of the behavior caused by the depression or start doing some of the healthier behaviors recommended here, it is time to make an appointment with a qualified medical professional.

In line with the assignment from Chapter One to increase socialization, start now to monitor and assess your social skills. Every time you leave a "social opportunity," which is basically an environment where there were people, score yourself with the Social Skill Assessment form. Photocopy the form and use it daily.

Social Skill Assessment

Depression influences our social skills, and these social skill deficits can worsen depression by the way they affect other people and reduce positive interpersonal exchanges. Use this scoring sheet to evaluate your social skills each time you leave a situation where there are "social opportunities." A social opportunity is any situation in which there is the possibility of some appropriate contact with someone else, such as an exchange of smiles, a brief verbal exchange, a conversation, or a compliment.

1. What Was the Social Situation? (e.g., dinner with friend, walking in mall, waiting in line at store, conversation on phone)

_____

2. What Were the Social Opportunities? (e.g., brief exchange, smile exchange, conversation)

_____

3. How'd You Do? (Circle or write down the social skills you accomplished. Review what was lacking and practice for next time)

a. Hygiene and Attire:
Clothes clean * Clothes unwrinkled * Clothes appropriate given social situation * Clothes attractive (coordinated, inviting colors, in style) * Hair combed or styled appropriately * Bathed/not malodorous * Shaved (for men) * Makeup (for women who wear it)

Others _____

b. Body Language/Mannerisms:
Good posture * Appropriate eye contact * Smiled * Laughed * Watched intonations * Changed expression to match changes in conversation * No distracting behaviors (nail biting, fidgeting, wringing hands) * Expression appropriate for tone of conversation * Facial movement

Others _____

c. Communication:
Appropriate tone * Appropriate volume * Appropriate rate * Responses given without long delay * Balance in give and take of conversation * Appropriate transitions * Kept talk about symptoms to minimum * Asked questions * Initiated conversation * Followed conversation; didn't zone out * Complimented * Avoided overly negative focus/cynicism * Did not leave too quickly/linger too long

Others _____

Main Points

1. Depression influences social skills. Social skill deficits are most apparent in severe depression, but even mildly depressed people will usually have some deficiencies in the skills necessary for smooth positive interactions. Individuals who have had chronic depression and severe social skill deficits or social phobia should try the techniques given here, but may need to seek out a behaviorally oriented clinician for more help.

2. It is important to try to improve social skills during depression, because social skill deficits can negatively influence relationships and actually push people away. People can be medicinal, and positive social interactions can increase the patches of relief so necessary for breaking depression.

3. Three important social skill areas are hygiene and attire, body language, and verbal communication. People with depression should make an effort to bathe, dress, and style their hair just as they did before they were depressed. People with depression may not be aware that they are using body language that keeps other people away, and should try to practice mirroring the mannerisms and body language of non-depressed people around them. Verbal communication may become awkward and slowed, and people with depression are encouraged to try to practice mirroring the vocal tone of their partners, to initiate more, to avoid talking too much about negative topics and themselves, and to pay more attention to the give-and-take of conversation.

4. The social skill assessment form can be used as a grading tool after a social event. With the form, users can congratulate themselves for the social skills they are attempting to implement, and be reminded of the ones they need to practice.

Chapter Seven:

Anxiety: Depression's Ugly Little Friend

Anxiety is a significant part of many depressed people's experience and dealing with it can be an important part of defeating depression. Anxiety is the most common psychiatric complaint. More people go to their doctor because of anxiety than for coughs and colds (Marshland, Wood, & Mayo, 1976). Research has consistently demonstrated a strong correlation between anxiety and depression. In excellent reviews of research by Clark (1989) and Gotlib and Cane (1989), it was found that the higher someone scores on a standardized depression inventory, the higher that person tends to score on a standardized anxiety inventory.

But just because anxiety is popular doesn't mean it wins any beauty contests. Just as Richard's depressive ogre is ugly, the anxiety ogre is ugly, plus it's one heck of a menace.

Depression & anxiety can be inseperable companions.

As if depression wasn't enough, adding anxiety to the hopper doubles the distress. Prolonged anxiety problems can disrupt work, interpersonal relationships, and sleep. When anxiety reaches the heights of panic, it can be debilitating. What a terrible little creep anxiety is. The depressive ogre and anxiety make a malevolent pair indeed.

For many depressed people, anxiety is the most subjectively distressing symptom. In fact, people with anxious depressions are often prescribed an anti-anxiety, or "anxiolytic," medication to go along with their antidepressant. The newer serotonin selective antidepressants can also be helpful for anxiety.

Pieces of Anxiety

Cognitive therapy lends itself quite well to anxiety. Like depression, anxiety has emotional, physical, cognitive, and behavioral symptoms, some of which are targetable with cognitive techniques. You know that with the cognitive approach to depression, you identify and stop the symptoms that keep the depression going; now let's look at how that same approach works with anxiety.

The *emotional* component of anxiety is fear. By anyone's definition, fear is a painful urgent emotion, like some uninvited high voltage current running through you. It's dreadful. There are different levels of fearful mood. Nervousness is used to describe low-level anxious mood, whereas panic is a profound blast of anxiety.

The *physical* symptoms of anxiety are myriad and they include shortness of breath, rapid heart rate, shakiness, dizziness, unsteadiness, numbness and tingling, lightheadedness, feelings of choking, and sweating. It is very hard to ignore the physical symptoms of anxiety. People with panic disorder misinterpret or "catastrophize" these physical symptoms. This "fear of fear" compounds anxiety to the point of making the person feel paralyzed or unable to move.

In terms of *cognitive* symptoms, anxiety strongly influences attention. Focus becomes narrowly directed, or "hypervigilant," toward the danger cues in the environment (e.g., Burgess, Jones, Robertson, Radcliffe, Emerson, Lawler, & Crow, 1981; Parkinson & Rachman, 1981). With some forms of anxiety, for example, phobia, the danger is outside the self, whereas with other manifestations of anxiety, such as panic disorder, the danger is for the most part internal. Anxiety seems to hog all the thinking space (what is referred to as cognitive capacity) leaving little left to encode, store and retrieve information. (MacLoed & Mathews (1991) offer a great summary of the research in this area). An anxious person just can't think of anything but what he is anxious about! An anxious person's automatic thoughts and mental images tend to be "catastrophic"; that is, anxious individuals inflate the possibility of a disastrous outcome (e.g. Butler & Mathews, 1987).

So, basically, when anxiety hits, all systems go on disaster alert: paralyzing emotion, intense bodily sensations, narrowly focused attention, and catastrophic thoughts. It's like every bit of you is screaming Warning! Warning! Attention becomes so narrowly focused on whatever is causing the anxiety that you can barely think of anything else, see the situation as far worse than it really is, and feel that you have no control over what is happening. This quite rapid activation of symptoms has one *behavioral* purpose: flight. This is without a doubt the most important mechanism in terms of survival that we have in the circuitry of our brains. If the tremendously uncomfortable experience of anxiety didn't happen in the face of danger, we'd all perish for sure. Anxiety alerts us to danger and makes us more likely to escape from it. Quickly.

However, some people experience an inappropriate level of anxiety given the dangerousness of the situation or have enduring anxiety despite a relatively safe environment. Anxiety problems can be described as false alarms that are too frequent, too profound, or too prolonged given the dangers at hand.

Anxiety problems are self-perpetuating, mostly by virtue of cognitive distortions and the overuse of flight/avoidance strategies. Consider Joe, who quit his job as a bartender due to severe anxiety. He's been out of work for a month. A friend orchestrates a job interview for Joe, but the night before, Joe begins catastrophizing big time. Therefore, he's experiencing a considerable amount of anxious mood and unpleasant physical symptoms. The more anxious Joe gets, the more catastrophic he thinks. Joe is thinking, "I will fail; they won't hire me; I won't be able to handle the anxiety of the interview." Joe becomes such a blazing ball of anxiety that he can't stand it any more, and he elects to cancel the interview. Joe feels relief.

The relief part here is important. Joe's decision to blow off the opportunity communicated to his brain that all the catastrophic predictions he was having were no longer going to happen. So his brain turned off the anxious alarm system. To use behavioral terminology, Joe's decision to cancel was "negatively reinforcing." The next time Joe is offered an interview, he will not only be likely to catastrophize and

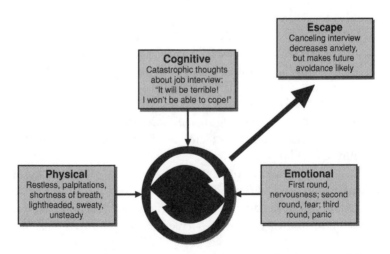

As with depression, the symptoms of anxiety feed the condition.

experience considerable anxiety, but he will also be strongly compelled to cancel the interview again. After several such scenarios, Joe becomes stuck in an anxiety/avoidance cycle that is very difficult to get out of.

Getting a Grip on Anxiety: Where Are the Handles?

Despite its all-consuming nature, it is possible to gain control over anxiety. There are many ways to manage anxiety. Let's look at them, grouped by symptoms: emotional, physical, cognitive, and behavioral.

Emotional Symptoms: Cognitive therapy techniques don't focus directly on emotions. They hit thinking, which in turn, modifies emotion. Medicines can directly target the emotional symptoms of anxiety. For example, the benzodiazapines influence some of the neurotransmitters responsible for anxious mood (as well as the physical symptoms), as do some of the serotonin antidepressants. A sound pharmacological regime is often a necessary part of treatment for anxious individuals. However, psychiatrists are usually mindful not to have their patients use sedating medications as the sole means of dealing with anxiety, because some people may come to depend exclusively on the medication to the point that the medications are overused, or may find that using anxiolytic medication on an as-needed basis becomes an escape strategy in and of itself.

Physical Symptoms: It is literally impossible to be anxious and relaxed at the same time. Therefore, skills for promoting relaxation are very powerful in reducing anxiety. Progressive muscle relaxation is a method designed to teach people how to recognize involuntary muscle tension and to relax muscle groups. It involves sequentially tightening and relaxing muscle groups, starting with the feet and legs and moving upward to the neck and face. There are many audiotapes available that walk people through this technique, and I've found most to be quite good, even if they tend to vary a lot with regard to the specific muscle groups. Some therapists advocate the technique as an "in and of itself" method of relaxing. Though this is true, the purpose of progressive muscle relaxation is to help people train their brain to know the difference between muscle tension and deep relaxation. After several weeks of regular pairing of the two opposite states, many people can cue themselves into relaxation when stressful tension occurs in their lives.

The diaphragmatic breathing technique, which we will look at in detail shortly, is an exercise that reduces the rate and increases the depth of breathing to promote relaxation. With considerable practice, anxious individuals can learn to slow down their breathing during bouts of anxiety.

Visualization techniques are aimed at helping people bring about a relaxed physical state by conjuring up vivid and soothing experiences and fantasies. Again, there are many excellent guided imagery audiotapes available in pharmacies, health stores, and bookstores.

Cognitive Symptoms: Cognitive skills for managing anxiety involve *distraction* and *decatastrophizing*. Distraction is a very powerful means of reducing intense anxiety and panic. When someone is consumed with a high level of anxiety, it is very hard to recognize and challenge distorted thoughts. However, if anxiety-stricken people can "get out of their heads" for a few minutes by focusing intensely and exclusively on some outside stimulus (while at the same time using the diaphragmatic breathing method), the distraction will cause their anxiety to diminish, often to a level where they can reason with themselves. Decatastrophizing is a disputation technique aimed at balancing exaggerated automatic thoughts. As we did with the hopeless, helpless, and worthless thoughts of depression, we want to dispute the exaggerated thoughts that drive anxiety. Decatastrophizing, as you will see, involves re-examining whatever it is we're anxious about so it doesn't seem like such a terrible emergency; carving mountains back into molehills, as it were.

Behavioral symptoms: Escape, avoidance, and procrastination are understandable responses to the excruciating experience of anxiety. Unfortunately, the relief is short-lived, but the negative consequences creep in and build strength until they are like an impenetrable fortress. The more someone avoids things that make him anxious, the harder it is not to keep on avoiding them. With each successful escape or avoidance, the brain rewards the person with relief. Our brains are designed to compel us toward behaviors that in the past have resulted in a decrease in anxiety. At a primal level, relief spells safety. Our brains aren't too concerned with whether what is being avoided is truly dangerous. We've evolved with a higher likelihood to make false positives than false negatives when it comes to danger (better safe than sorry). Our brains are primarily interested in getting us to react to immediate dangers; they aren't as concerned with the long-term consequence of avoidance and escape, which is perpetuation of anxiety and depression.

The remedy is simple: if you are anxious, you need to stop avoiding things that make you anxious and expose yourself to your fears. Sure. Simple. Right. The reality is that exposure is simple in theory but excruciating to implement. It can feel like barreling unarmed into the fray. However, nothing rivals it in terms of decreasing anxiety problems in a long-term way. The panic disordered person needs to stay in the grocery until the panic goes away completely. The person with performance anxiety must socialize and mingle. The person with a phobia about snakes must hold a snake (that is, if he actually wants to reduce this fear).

We will look later at systematic desensitization, which involves creating an upward staircase of gradually increasing levels of anxiety. Some people with anxiety that is not debilitating can create such a staircase on their own. People with severe anxiety problems should seek out a behaviorally oriented anxiety specialist. Countering avoidance is the greatest challenge to a person with anxiety, and the supportive push of an expert makes it a lot more likely that the person will actually follow through with exposure.

Reducing High Anxiety and Panic

If you are in a state of panic or super high anxiety, the Thought Record Flow Sheet exercise is out of the question. You're just too anxious. Metacognition literally freezes in such states. There are, however, two things that you can do: alter your breathing and redirect your attention. Diaphragmatic breathing is a method of slowing and deepening breathing that has a direct effect on anxiety. Remember, anxiety and relaxation are mutually exclusive states. Bringing about a relaxed physical state reduces anxiety.

Anti-anxiety Breaths and Distraction

Here's how you do it: sit comfortably with your feet on the floor, then place the palm of your hand over your diaphragm. Breathe in deeply through your nose to the count of four, to the extent that you can feel your belly rising. Hold to the count of four, and then exhale to the count of six. Do this three or four times, then just breathe in a steady relaxed manner. Diaphragmatic breathing only works if you can add distraction. Otherwise, you'll just keep thinking horrible thoughts and when you stop deep breathing, go right back to hyperventilation. The hyper-focus on internal symptoms and catastrophic thoughts keeps anxiety on the rise. However, if you can distract yourself by getting truly absorbed in something outside of you, without checking back to the internal symptoms, anxiety drops.

Counting objects can be a good distraction: you can count light bulbs, lines on the wall, Venetian blinds, leaves on the house plant, specks of crud on the carpet, gum wads on the sidewalk, stars in the sky. External distractions work best, but some people can fully distract themselves with something in their own head that is neutral, such as a poem, a song, a pleasant "memory video" of playing water polo, planting apple seeds, or doing piggyback square dancing at last year's hoedown. A good internal distraction is to envision the numbers you count while breathing diaphragmatically. Go wild with them, like they do on children's television programs: animate them, morph them into flowers, change colors and patterns.

I understand that distracting yourself when you're anxious is very hard to do. It will take practice for you to become efficient at completely removing yourself from what is going on internally. When I say practice, I mean several times a day.

Self-Talk

It's virtually impossible to reason with yourself when you are consumed with high anxiety. Once you've been able to reduce your anxiety to a moderate or mild level with distraction and diaphragmatic breathing, you can then use metacognition in the same way you are using it to decrease depression by countering Big Bad Thoughts. As opposed to hopeless, helpless, or worthless thoughts, we want to hack away at catastrophic exaggerations.

Unlike depression, which is for the most part a stable state that gives you opportunities to sit down and complete a thought record, anxiety comes on like a fist blow, often in places where you can't whip out a pencil and paper and start completing a Thought Record Flow Sheet, such as in a stressful meeting with your boss or while you're waiting in line at the grocery store. Remember, you carry metacognition with you at all times, and talking to yourself can bring anxiety down. People who manage stressful situations engage in a form of coping called self-talk, where, basically, they talk themselves (not out loud, but in their heads) out of being anxious.

There are four themes of decatastrophizing self-talk:

1. *This is temporary.* When you are in an anxiety-provoking situation, it feels like it's never going to end. Reminding yourself that all events are time-limited can reduce anxiety significantly. An example might be if you say, "Okay, this job interview is only going to be an hour long at most. I can handle an hour of discomfort. An hour of discomfort is not as bad as two hours of discomfort."

2. *I've handled similar or worse events in the past.* Anxiety creates amnesia for past coping. Remind yourself of the stressors in the past that you have been able to overcome. In particular, remind yourself of ones that were at least as overwhelming as the current one. An example might be, "Okay, this job interview is definitely important, but I'll get through it. I got through my licensing oral examination, and that was several times as excruciating as this."

3. *This isn't so terrible.* Anxiety disorders are differentiated from normal high states of anxiety by virtue of how reasonable the anxiety is given the danger at hand. To have a panic attack under the jaws of a saber-toothed tiger would be reasonable. Saber-toothed tigers are dangerous. To have a panic attack during a lunch meeting with colleagues is not reasonable. Unless these colleagues are wielding pistols, they are not likely to hurt you. Argue that the danger at hand is not that dangerous by comparing it to things that are truly dangerous. This puts the event at hand into perspective. Say to yourself, "Okay, this interviewer is in a position to hire me or not. Certainly this is a powerful position, but even if the worst-case scenario occurs and he doesn't hire me, he cannot hurt me. If I were negotiating my life with some alley thug right now, that would be dangerous. This guy's just some stranger with a bad tie who will either hire me or not."

4. *I have some control over this situation.* When we are anxious, we think we have the power of a soap bubble. Reminding yourself of your resources in the heat of the moment can really kill anxiety. It can also be helpful to remind yourself of escape hatches, not that you should necessarily use them, but simply to acknowledge that they are there. Tell yourself, "I have a very impressive resume, plus a degree. I earned these things, which puts me in a position to be sitting in this interview right now. I'm interviewing him, too. If I don't like what he has to offer, I don't have to take it."

Another method of self-talk is *cognitive exposure*. This method, which involves the consideration of worst-case scenarios, is useful for worrisome situations in which there is a chance of a moderately negative outcome. It is *not* advocated for situations in which there is a remote chance of something extremely catastrophic, such as death, terminal illness, prison time, or living on the street, as this technique will only lead to increased worrying and catastrophizing. Some appropriate events for cognitive exposure would be returning to work, being assertive with your boss, dropping a class, or attending a job interview. Cognitive exposure involves, first, thinking in a very vivid way about the worst potential outcome, then walking through the steps as to what you'd really do about it if it actually happened. Though this technique might sound like ordinary worrying, it is quite different. Worrying is a self-protective strategy we engage in to prevent worst-case scenarios. With cognitive exposure, you are actually placing yourself in the situation mentally and coping with it. In your mind, there is no way you can prevent it, because it has already happened. Anxiety reduction comes from mentally walking through the steps by asking yourself, "Then what?" after each imagined decision. Almost invariably, you will end up realizing that though it may be undesirable, the worst-case scenario won't kill you.

For example, let's say Joe gets invited back to his job as a bartender. He's terribly worried that it isn't going to work out. Cognitive exposure would involve thinking about the worst-case scenario, such as "having to quit," actually occurring. Joe is now in a position where he must do something. Here's a transcript of Joe's successful cognitive exposure: "What would I do? Heck, I'd cry. Then what? I'd call friends for support. Then what? I'd probably receive support. Then what? In several days I'll start looking for another job—I always manage to find work and I have good interview skills. Then what? I'd check out work in a part of town closer to home. Then what? I'd eventually get job, possibly a less stressful job."

In some instances, such as in Joe's situation, worst-case scenarios can even yield positive outcomes. The next step of cognitive exposure is to conjure up vividly the best-case scenario. It is important to focus on worst case first, as best case will seem completely impossible until you've convinced yourself you can handle the worst case. In Joe's case, the best-case scenario might be returning to work and finding things to be considerably less stressful due to changes initiated by his boss and Joe's own improved stress management skills.

After imaging both worst and best potential outcomes, the logical conclusion is that all outcomes in between could be managed; however, as a third step, entertaining one or two realistic-case scenarios places you in a balanced state of mind. Again, it isn't until the most terrible outcome is "exorcised" that the more likely realistic outcomes can be entertained in a believable way. Referring to Barkeep Joe again, a realistic outcome for him might be returning to find things a bit less stressful at work due to his increased ability to manage stress and approaching the first week on the job as a trial period during which other job opportunities will be investigated, so that if things end up being overwhelming, Joe can make a smooth transition.

As with depression, the more you practice metacognition to fight anxiety, the more automatic it will become.

Reducing the Gap

Since the late 1960s, Richard Lazarus and his colleagues have contributed considerably to our understanding of stress and cognitive appraisal (e.g., Lazarus, 1966; Lazarus & Launier, 1978; Lazarus & Folkman, 1984). Lazarus proposed the existence of two appraisal systems: a primary appraisal, which is our judgment about a situation (is it safe, positive, irrelevant, stressful?); and a secondary appraisal system (what can I do about it?). He concluded that stress will be considerable when primary appraisals of stress, such as threat, challenge, harm or loss, are coupled with secondary appraisals in which the individual feels he can do little or nothing to cope with it.

Inspired by Lazarus' work on stress, I have found it very helpful to patients grappling with anxiety to be able to break down their anxiety into two distinct appraisals. I explain to patients that at the root of every anxious moment are two perceptions: one relating to the danger at hand, and the other relating to their control over that danger. When your perception of control is in line with your perception of danger, and you believe that you have sufficient control to manage the danger at hand, anxiety is absent. However, if your perception of control is not in line with your perception of danger, and you believe that you do not have sufficient control to manage the danger, anxiety will be present.

For example, imagine you're downtown, and there is an intoxicated shirtless thug barreling down the sidewalk toward you with a nasty scowl on his face and a crowbar in his hand. Now, most of us would deem that a pretty dangerous event. However, it's the middle of the day, and there are three muscle-bound vigilantes walking right in front of you, plus a row of open doors parallel to the sidewalk leading into the police station, plus you are a triple black belt in Tai Quan Do. Here, the danger is reduced by the tools you have to deal with it, and you would not be very anxious.

However, let's change the time of day to 3 A.M., lose the vigilantes, put "closed" signs on all the police station doors, and put a cast on your leg and give you crutches. Now we have a considerably more dangerous situation over which you have less control. As a result, you have some pretty intense anxiety.

So, basically, the level of anxiety we experience is less a matter of specific dangers and specific controls than it is the "distance" between how we view the danger and how we think we can cope with it. The greater the gap between our perception of danger and our perception of control, the greater the anxiety. Moving away from the example of menacing thugs and broken legs, we could imagine the *danger* of a job interview, with perceptions of hostile interviewers with impossible questions, and perceiving our *control* over the interview as next to nil, in that there will be an inability to respond, combined with anxiety, tearfulness, or possible fainting. Here, though the actual situation would seem by most to be less dangerous, the gap could result in a level of anxiety on par with the example involving thugs and crutches.

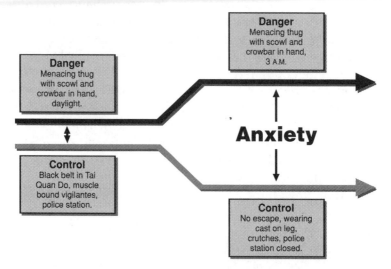

The gap between how dangerous you think a situation is and how much control you have over it determines the amount of anxiety you have. The larger the gap, the higher the anxiety.

The Decatastrophizing Exercize

Following is a special Thought Record Flow Sheet , called the Decatastrophizing Worksheet. It is designed to help you reduce anxiety by reducing the gap between how you see the danger and how you see your ability to control it. The Decatastrophizing Worksheet is based on the view that anxiety comes from a combination of beliefs of exaggerated danger and minimized control. The Decatastrophizing Worksheet, you'll notice, has more steps than the Thought Record Flow Sheet, but really, it's just like doing two flow sheets. One tests the evidence for the belief that you are being confronted with terrible danger and the other tests

Few would argue that this is not a high-danger situation.

the belief that you have minimal or no control over that danger.

Here's how you do it. First, write down the situation that is causing you anxiety, for example, a job interview, marital problems, or that final exam tomorrow. Second, rate your anxiety on the same 0-100 percent scale as was used on the Thought Record Flow Sheet. Then attempt to translate this stressor into two beliefs: one about the danger of the situation, and the other about your level of control over it. With regard to "final exam tomorrow" the two thoughts might read: "The test will be impossible" and "I'll fail miserably and there's nothing I can do about it." Now you want to use the test of evidence strategy illustrated in Chapter Four for each of these beliefs. List evidence supporting your belief that the danger is excessive, then use the Dr. Frankenstein technique to help you find evidence that disputes the thought. Remember, the Dr. Frankenstein Technique entails building someone or some situation, piece by piece, that would be totally dangerous. This technique helps bring to mind aspects of your situation that are not that bad. Do the same with your belief about not having control: list evidence supporting this claim, then bring out old Franky again and create someone so ill-equipped and vulnerable that they literally have no control and are the epitome of helplessness. What will typically come to mind are attributes and support systems and safety nets you hadn't thought about before. It is recommended you practice "Reducing the Gap" regularly. Though this may sound like a broken record by now, remember, the only way cognitive skills can have a measurable effect on mood is if you do them a lot.

That Nasty Word: Exposure

If people want to reduce their anxiety, it is essential that they stop avoiding situations that make them anxious. Avoiding anxiety-producing situations reduces anxiety in the short term, but it actually makes for more anxiety in the long term. Avoidance breeds more avoidance, and it becomes increasingly difficult to break out of that cycle. Again, giving Joe the spotlight, if he catastrophizes returning to work so much that he becomes extremely anxious, he may choose to postpone it. This will decrease his anxiety now, but will make it even harder to return the next day, because not only will he have increased anxiety just considering going back to work, but he will have a strong drive to postpone again, since postponing going back to work last time decreased his anxiety.

Exposure involves placing yourself in the situation you want to avoid, despite the anxiety, and staying there until the anxiety ebbs completely. Most people with severe anxiety shun exposure because the anxiety actually gets worse before it diminishes. The help of an experienced therapist is recommended if you are unable to counter avoidance on your own.

A method called systematic desensitization (Wolpe, 1958) can help with most forms of anxiety. Just as the name implies, the idea is just to get used to something, or desensitized, gradually. With this approach, the person gradually exposes him or herself to what has been avoided, starting with a level that causes very little anxiety and applying relaxation and

Decatastrophizing Worksheet (Example)

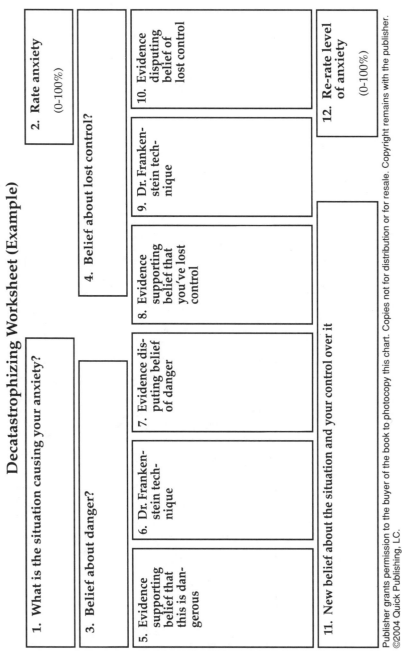

1. What is the situation causing your anxiety?

2. Rate anxiety
(0-100%)

3. Belief about danger?

4. Belief about lost control?

5. Evidence supporting belief that this is dangerous

6. Dr. Frankenstein technique

7. Evidence disputing belief of danger

8. Evidence supporting belief that you've lost control

9. Dr. Frankenstein technique

10. Evidence disputing belief of lost control

11. New belief about the situation and your control over it

12. Re-rate level of anxiety
(0-100%)

Decatastrophizing Worksheet (Example)

1. What is the situation causing your anxiety?

Overwhelming job stress!

2. Rate anxiety
(0-100%) **75%**

3. Belief about danger?

My job is totally unbearable.

4. Belief about lost control?

There is nothing I can do about it.

5. Evidence supporting belief that this is dangerous

Workload has increased. Boss has written me up twice. I don't enjoy my job the way I used to. I had to take a leave of absence due to stress and depression.

6. Dr. Frankenstein technique

A totally unbearable job. All demands would be in excess of my abilities. I'd be hated by everyone, making mistake upon mistake, having a totally inflexible boss. Plus, it would be unbearable whether I was depressed or not.

7. Evidence disputing belief of danger

I used to do okay before the stress and depression hit. I'm working on getting out of this bog. Plus, there are opportunities to reconcile the problems (different duties). I haven't approached my boss. Other jobs in town given my skills if problems endure.

8. Evidence supporting belief that you've lost control

I pushed myself to the point of having to go into the hospital. My efforts at easing problems have not been successful. Too many problems at home make it impossible to concentrate at work.

9. Dr. Frankenstein technique

Someone completely help-less would be without job skills. He would have no support at all. He would have exhausted every option. He'd have an intractable mental illness, and he'd have a history of solving problems like this in the past.

10. Evidence disputing belief of lost control

My wife and I are working together to solve problems. We've managed in the past. Friends have been support-ive too. Haven't talked to boss about assignment change. I'm doing something about the depression. Once that's gone, I'll be back to my old self.

11. New belief about the situation and your control over it

My job seems more stressful due to many concurrent stressors. I'm working on diminishing these other problems and getting out of this depression. There are opportunities to make work less stressful that I haven't pursued. I have the skills. If things don't change, I can certainly put feelers out for another job.

12. Re-rate level of anxiety
(0-100%) **40%**

cognitive coping responses. After each level becomes more comfortable and the anxiety is eliminated at that level, the exposure is increased. For example, consider someone with a snake phobia. This person might be exposed to photographs of snakes, and asked to look at them while using relaxation and decatastrophizing skills until the photos no longer cause anxiety. Then the person would be exposed to a realistic rubber snake, here touching it, holding it, while using relaxation and decatastrophizing skills until the anxiety diminishes completely. The next exposure step might involve a live snake in a locked aquarium, followed by more steps all the way up to holding a live harmless snake. Systematic desensitization as applied to the young fellow returning to work might have as an initial step driving around the parking lot of his job on a Sunday. That could be followed by talking to a colleague on the phone and visiting the workplace before his return date. Then he could start work part time and work his way back to full-time employment.

The reason anxiety is so manageable is that there are so many potentially effective ways to intervene. Though everyone is different as far as which methods are most effective, try practicing all the methods we've looked at. Remember, unlike skills for managing depression, some of the cognitive behavioral techniques designed to help you reduce anxiety necessarily cause an *increase* in anxiety before the anxiety starts heading out the door for good. It is important to continue with the techniques despite the temporary increase, as it is a necessary part of evicting this unwelcome creep. Using an exercise analogy, when someone who is out of shape begins to work out, it is typically excruciating, and there is often strong motivation to quit working out. If the person keeps with it, the workouts become easier, enjoyable even, as the person becomes more healthy, toned, and attractive.

Main Points

1. Anxiety is a nasty component of many people's depression. Depression feeds anxiety, and anxiety feeds depression. Controlling anxiety can remove what many find to be the most dreadfully painful part of depression.
2. Anxiety has emotional, physical, cognitive and behavioral symptoms. Just like depression, anxiety is a self-perpetuating state. The symptoms feed each other.
3. There are powerful medications that can reduce anxiety. Some depressed people, in addition to being prescribed an antidepressant, will also be prescribed an anti-anxiety, or anxiolytic, medication to help calm them. However, some antidepressants, in addition to reducing depression, can also reduce anxiety.
4. Physical symptoms can be targeted with medication as well as with diaphragmatic breathing and structured relaxation techniques. In very high states of anxiety, it is important to interrupt the shallow breathing. The diaphragmatic breathing technique is easy in theory, but requires daily practice to be truly effective.
5. In very high states of anxiety, you are not able to argue the legitimacy of catastrophic thoughts; indeed, often you can't even articulate the catastrophic thoughts. Distraction and diaphragmatic breathing combined can reduce profound anxiety in a short period of time. Moderate and mild levels of anxiety can be managed by decatastrophizing. You can decatastrophize in your head by self-talk and cognitive exposure. Regular use of the decatastrophizing thought record form can really help you hone the skill.
6. Avoidance is common among anxious people. Avoidance reduces anxiety only in the short term. The more one avoids the situation that causes anxiety, the more frightening exposure becomes. A technique to eliminate anxiety involves gradually increasing the level of exposure in stages, moving upward only after the last stage did not cause anxiety.

Chapter Eight:

Motivation: Talking Your Feet into Moving

Depression is like a weed problem; you have to suffocate every little shoot. If you leave even one, it will mature, then send its little seeds all over the yard. And shortly, after the next rain, you've got your weed problem again.

Depression is like any infestation; you must be diligent and thorough in order to eliminate it. It has already been hammered home that the cognitive strategies presented in this book won't help your depression at all unless you implement them regularly and integrate them into your days. And you have to keep at this stuff for a while even after your depression has lifted. Recovery from depression is very often fraught with lapses, dips, bad mornings, bad evenings, and bad days. The last thing you want to happen is to slip from a low mood lapse back into a full-fledged depressive relapse.

If you experience a lapse during your ascent from depression, and in response to it curl back into the sack and let Richard's ogre climb back on board, it's just like that nasty weed problem. The depression will get its foothold back, and thrive. Many people who undergo cognitive therapy are frustrated at how much daily work recovery requires. It is literally exhausting to be fighting against the pull to lie down, to avoid things that worry you and to isolate yourself from the world. It's exhausting to have to constantly catch and challenge the negative thoughts that keep cropping up even though you're fighting them. It is so easy to just say, "Forget it!" and start diving back down into the cave of depression like a defeated bat.

This chapter focuses on motivation enhancement. Motivation deserves an entire chapter, because, in my experience with depressed people, if the tools are not practiced and if behavioral changes are not implemented, depression can be prolonged. People who have somehow found the ability to move forward and practice the cognitive behavioral skills, despite the strong pull to do otherwise, are often able to get out of the depression quicker.

Taking action is difficult for someone who is grappling with depression. The lack of drive, feelings of apathy and low energy interfere with the ability to follow through with tasks vital for the reduction of depression. Also, ambivalence (that state in which you simultaneously like and don't like something, or want and don't want to do something) about using cognitive behavioral change techniques is common. Cognitive behavior therapists ask that their patients change what are sometimes longstanding or habitual patterns of thinking and behavior. It is natural not to just relinquish them without some apprehension.

(The strategies we are going to look at for increasing motivation are based on the pioneering work of Dr. William Miller, who developed a non-coercive style of helping individuals change addictive behavior, called motivational interviewing (Miller & Rollnick, 1991), as well as the Transtheoretical Model of Change, developed by James Prochaska, Ph.D., Carlo DiClemente, Ph.D. (1982), and Prochaska, Norcross and DiClemente (1994).)

What we want to do is to increase motivation to do things associated with feeling better, since our natural drive to do so is stuck in the tar pit of depression. Sometimes just telling yourself to put the "cart before the horse" or that "action precedes motivation" isn't going to be enough to get you off the sofa. So, as we've done to states of depression and anxiety in earlier chapters, low motivation and states of ambivalence will need to be broken down into tangible thoughts, beliefs, and predictions. Once identified, these beliefs can be examined for accuracy and altered if necessary.

Consider Melissa. She doesn't like being told what to do. She revealed that her mother had been very controlling and Melissa grew up to be quite sensitive to demands rendered by others, especially others who were in positions of authority. Melissa was very motivated to take part in the outpatient cognitive therapy program and boasted of having read lots of books on it before she came in, but the first time I asked her to do some self-monitoring, she said, "I'll think about it." Arguing with Melissa would have been futile, because this would have been construed as more mom-like mandating and she'd no doubt dig her heels in all the more. Instead, helping Melissa understand her ambivalence and helping her learn to use cognitive arguing tools to assess whether any of her thoughts and beliefs could be modified resulted in her moving forward with the recommendations for change.

I approached Melissa as though she was completely motivated to increase socialization, initiate pleasurable activities, and do the Thought Record Flow Sheet and the Thought Debate Exercise regularly. What I failed to understand was that, even though she desperately wanted to get out of depression, she had a great deal of ambivalence about the assignments due to the fact that they were coming from an authority figure.

Backing up and focusing on what submitting meant to her was much more fruitful than staying in a tug of war. She was able to identify several beliefs, such as "Giving into authority leads to shame," and "Authority figures are mean and insensitive." These beliefs were explored and aspects of them were challenged. Also, Melissa was able to help me understand that she would more likely follow through with a gentle approach to assignments and experiments in which she felt some modicum of control. Then, she was able to move forward.

Lots of ambivalent dilemmas occur when people are in cognitive behavior therapy. They may think things such as "I don't know if I should do these pencil and paper assignments," and "I'm not sure it will help me to increase my socialization," and "I don't think I should get out of bed because I'm just too tired."

Ambivalence in Balance

There are four cognitive components to any ambivalent dilemma, or a situation where you are stuck trying to decide what to do. Staying in bed is based on a rationale that includes pros, or positives, of staying in bed as well as cons, or negatives, associated with getting up. Likewise, getting up is based on our beliefs as to the pros associated with doing so as well as the cons associated with not doing so. Such dilemmas can be depicted with a seesaw, on which we have the cognitive components impeding change on one side, and the cognitive components driving change on the other. When we're unmotivated or ambivalent, the seesaw is level. Our goal is to see if we can tip the seesaw in favor of change.

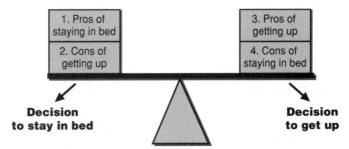

The decision to stay in bed or get up is made by balancing the pros and cons of each decision.

The decision to get up or stay in bed is based solely on the significance, or "cognitive weight," of one side versus the other. If the pros of staying in bed and the cons of getting up (the two quadrants on the left side) outweigh the pros of getting up and the cons of staying in bed (the two quadrants on the right side), the person will stay in bed, and vice versa.

The reasons a depressed person might stay in bed despite "knowing" that it would be better for him or her to get up and get moving is because the advantages of staying in bed seem more valid. This person may have lots of recent experience with staying in bed and "enjoyed" avoiding the anxiety of facing people and responsibilities, but very little recent experience getting up and feeling better as a consequence. Therefore, in order to get that person motivated, a convincing case must be made for doing so.

Tipping the Scale

To enhance motivation or tilt an ambivalent dilemma in favor of positive action, you must make a case for the healthier decision. To do this, you can apply certain cognitive strategies, most of which we've already discussed with regard to the Big Bad Thoughts of depression and the catastrophic ones of anxiety.

The first step is to list the beliefs for each component of the dilemma that's keeping you stuck. Keeping with the example of getting out of bed or staying in it, the pros of staying in bed might be avoiding feeling depressed, being asleep or "unconscious," avoiding the demands of the day, and getting rest. The cons of getting up might be having to face people, having to face problems, and having to feel depressed. Moving to the other side of the seesaw, you must try to conjure up reasons for the healthier choice. Reasons for getting up might be actually feeling better, having a positive social contact, having distraction from the depression, and ultimately breaking the depression. The cons of not getting up might include insomnia, guilt for having blown off a day, mounting unmet responsibilities and worsening depression.

Now that the information maintaining the stuck state is organized, it can be examined for accuracy and tinkered with.

The Three Ds

Tilting the balance will require making the rationale for staying in bed seem less attractive and making a better and more "real-feeling" rationale for getting up. You can do this using the cognitive tools of disputation, decatastrophizing, and dilation, called "the three Ds."

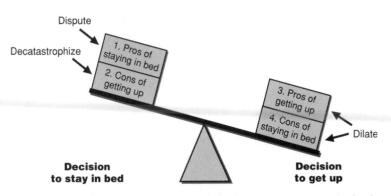

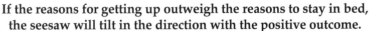

If the reasons for getting up outweigh the reasons to stay in bed, the seesaw will tilt in the direction with the positive outcome.

The first quadrant: The predicted pros of an unhealthy decision (like spending the day in bed). These beliefs tend to be distortions. Unlike distortions of depression, which are exaggerated in the negative direction, these distortions tend to be exaggerated in the positive direction; that is, we fool ourselves into thinking the benefits are absolutely fabulous and necessary. Using the disputation questions presented for countering depressive thoughts, the challenge here is to balance overly positive predictions by bringing the associated negatives into mind.

Dispute. Where's the evidence that what you've listed are truly benefits? Are they benefits with costs? Are there other ways of achieving the same benefits?

Avoiding the depression
Dispute: *The problems are only temporarily avoided.*

Being unconscious instead of depressed
Dispute: *Again, this is temporary; it doesn't help the depression go away in the long run and actually may prolong it.*

Avoiding the demands of the day
Dispute: *There will be new demands tomorrow to add to the ones I avoided today.*

Getting rest
Dispute: *I don't need all this rest. This is a symptom of depression. If I continue to give into it, I'll continue to stay depressed.*

The second quadrant: The predicted cons of making the healthy decision. These predictions tend to be fueled by fear and anxiety. The negatives are almost always worse in your mind than in reality. Put these predictions into perspective. Some negative predictions, when realized, actually end up offering positive opportunities.

Decatastrophize. What's the worst thing that can happen? Can I handle it? How? What's the best thing that can happen if I endure it? What's the most realistic outcome?

Having to face people
Decatastrophize: *I may be anxious and uncomfortable, but it won't hurt me. I may have a positive encounter even.*

Having to face problems
Decatastrophize: *They have to be faced. If I don't face them, they'll get worse. My predictions are always worse than how things actually pan out.*

Having to feel depressed
Decatastrophize: *I already am depressed. It's doubtful that I'll feel better lying here. I may wake up feeling worse. Often I've gotten moving and have felt better.*

The excruciating pain of putting together an outfit, showering, etc.
Decatastrophize: *There is nothing inherently painful about choosing clothing. It's just uncomfortable. I've handled things ten times as uncomfortable as choosing clothing.*

The third quadrant: The predicted pros of the healthy decision. Now moving to the right side of the seesaw, we want to dilate this data; that is, to exaggerate it and make it multi-sensory to feel as real as the data on the left side of the seesaw.

Dilate. Imagine as many positive outcomes as you can that might come from your action. Use as much detail as you can muster. Vividly conjure up a memory of engaging in this behavior and actually feeling better.

The fourth quadrant: Predicted cons of making an unhealthy decision. Here, you want to make vivid in your mind the disadvantages of not moving forward and the negative consequences, in this example, of languishing in bed. It is important to note that with the last quadrant, the cons

---

Improvement in mood
Dilate: *Remembering the day I got up, went with the family to get the Christmas tree and decorated it. I actually laughed that evening.*

Having a positive social contact
Dilate: *Remembering the time my friend wrenched me out of bed despite my depression. We ended up seeing a movie and I felt noticeably better.*

Having distractions from the depression
Dilate: *Getting involved in something is an effective distraction, like when I sat down and got some bills paid. Though not a particularly pleasurable task, it got my mind off of myself and I did feel better for finally getting the bills in the mail.*

Ultimately breaking the depression
Dilate: *Thinking vividly about how great it would be to finally get out of depression for good, the things I will be doing, and that decisions like this are necessary for recovery.*

---

of not making a healthy decision, thinking of bad things that might happen if they don't change their behavior can certainly motivate some people. However, this makes some other people feel worse. By all means complete this exercise, but if you find this occurring, it's okay to skip this quadrant, or to not give it as much emphasis as the others.

    Dilate. Imagine these negative things occurring if you continue avoiding action. Imagine them as vividly as possible.

Insomnia that night
Dilate: *Whenever I sleep all day, I toss and turn all night. Being awake and depressed in the middle of the night is the worst.*

Guilt for having blown off a day
Dilate: *I remember the day I didn't call in to work. I was bottled up all day with dread and misery.*

Mounting unmet responsibilities
Dilate: *I'll get that stinging, gnawing worry of unmet responsibilities, plus I'll get a crop of new ones that will soon be piled on top of the old ones.*

Worsening depression
Dilate: *What if I feel this depressed a month from now? I'm reminding myself that continuing to behave this way makes it likelier the depression will hang around.*

Seemingly small decisions, like Linda's decision to visit the park instead of staying in bed, can actually "immobilize" depression for prolonged periods.

Below is a Tipping the Scale form that Melissa completed, as well as a blank form for you to copy and use when faced with low motivation or other ambivalent dilemmas. Some other opportunities to use this exercise include: going back to work, being assertive with a spouse, cutting down or giving up alcohol, exercising, saving money, attending a social gathering, calling an estranged family member, completing the Thought Record Flow Sheet exercise, or making a lifestyle change.

This technique, though time-consuming, can be very powerful in helping you make changes for the better. With time, you will find that translating your conflicts into the four quadrants and applying the three Ds is something you can do in your head. You may also find that you don't always need to address all the quadrants in order to tip the scale. Sometimes it's just one culprit quadrant that is blocking healthy behavior. For Melissa, the culprit quadrant was "cons of doing the cognitive exercises," which included catastrophic predictions of being overpowered by authority and being treated insensitively, plus memories of previous tyrannical authority figures. Decatastrophizing these ideas was just the ticket.

Tipping the Scale Exercise

Left Side of Seesaw: The Unhealthy Decision

Pros of	Dispute
1.	1.
2.	2.
3.	3.
4.	4.
5.	5.
6.	6.

Cons of	Decatastrophize
1.	1.
2.	2.
3.	3.
4.	4.
5.	5.
6.	6.

Right Side of Seesaw: The Unhealthy Decision

Pros of	Dilate
1.	1.
2.	2.
3.	3.
4.	4.
5.	5.
6.	6.

Cons of	Dilate
1.	1.
2.	2.
3.	3.
4.	4.
5.	5.
6.	6.

Tipping the Scale Exercise
(Melissa's Example)

Left Side of Seesaw: The Unhealthy Decision

Pros of *Avoiding cog exercises*

1. *I get to just lie in bed all day instead; get more rest.*
2. *I get to avoid dealing with painful material that will make me feel bad.*
3. *I get to remain in control; not be told what to do.*

Dispute

1. *Lying in bed when depressed makes it worse.*
2. *Avoidance prolongs my depression. Plus, the outcome might be improved mood.*
3. *Not accepting help and guidance from others has only left me feeling alone and helpless with this depression.*

Cons of *Doing cog exercises*

1. *It will be taxing on my concentration.*
2. *It might not work.*
3. *I'll feel like a child doing his homework, giving in to authority, which I hate.*

Decatastrophize

1. *Yeah, because I'm depressed. That's normal.*
2. *I need to be open to trying whatever is available. It's new, but it might help me, and if not, I'll have to try several. If it still doesn't help, then I need additional help.*
3. *I may feel that way, but if it helps, then it's worth the temporary discomfort. It won't kill me. I let memories of my past interfere with current relationships, and I want to change that.*

Right Side of Seesaw: The Unhealthy Decision

Pros of *Doing cog exercises*

1. *Might feel less depressed.*
2. *Might increase my sense of hope.*
3. *Might increase my sense of control over this depression.*

Dilate

1. *I'm thinking vividly about eventually getting out of this depression, about how every little patch of relief weakens it.*
2. *I'm thinking vividly about having evidence that there's a light at the end of the tunnel.*
3. *I'm thinking vividly about the snowball effect of feeling more capable in terms of getting back to a productive life.*

Cons of *Avoiding cog exercises*

1. *Continued/worsening depression.*
2. *Possibly another missed opportunity to gain some control over this depression and getting back to a pleasurable life.*

Dilate

1. *I'm thinking vividly about how terrible it would be to have this depression go on and on, how not addressing the symptoms, like negative thinking, regularly, can prolong depression.*
2. *I'm thinking about lost time if depression continues to go unchecked.*

Main Points

1. Depressed people have a very difficult time motivating themselves. Though it is going to be impossible to bring about an enormous amount of motivation when we are in the throes of depression, what we need is just enough motivation to get ourselves up and moving and utilizing cognitive and behavioral skills frequently.
2. A theory of motivation that is borrowed from the realm of addictive behavior treatment can help us understand how ambivalence can stall our forward progress. The theory breaks down low-motivation and ambivalent situations into their cognitive parts.
3. A seesaw with four quadrants is used to depict a stuck state; on the left side are beliefs driving avoidance and unhealthy behaviors. The beliefs fall into two parts: the pros of engaging in the unhealthy behavior and the cons of not engaging in the unhealthy behavior. On the right side of the seesaw are placed beliefs driving a healthy decision. Those are also shown in two parts: the pros of engaging in the healthy behavior and the cons of continuing to engage in the unhealthy behavior.
4. The three Ds, which are dispute, decatastrophize, and dilate, are cognitive strategies used to target distortions in each of the quadrants on the seesaw. Successful restructuring of exaggerated, deficient, and catastrophic beliefs often tips the scale, and increases motivation to stop unhealthy behaviors or to engage in behaviors that will help reduce depression.

Chapter Nine:

Moderate Anger: Somewhere between Implosion and Explosion

Anger is an interesting emotion. By most people's definition, it is a negative emotion, but unlike other negative emotions, such as anxiety, it doesn't drive people away from its source. Anger makes people want to move toward the thing that angered them and get in its face. Anger is an "expansive" state that drives action toward its reduction. Many people with depression also have problems with anger, and the two mood states can fuel each other in a most unsavory manner.

Like a balloon filling rapidly with hot air, anger creates an urgency to "do something" before it pops. Like anxiety, anger can be very difficult to control because of its abrupt onset and all-consuming nature. As with depression and anxiety, it is useful to break down the experience into its four symptom categories so the tangible aspects can be identified.

The *emotional* component of anger is referred to as "madness." The words "frustration" and "rage" best define the two extremes of angry mood.

In terms of *physical* symptoms, anger increases blood pressure. Restlessness and muscle tension occur. People vary in terms of where they tighten up. For some, tension is in the jaw or brow; for others, the shoulders and back will become taut; some find themselves clenching their fists. Many people become flushed when angry; in fact, anger is sometimes described as "heating up." When a person is angry, there is a significant burst in adrenaline. A person can be completely spent from a long day at work and dozing off, then, when provoked, can find himself bouncing off the walls with energy and venom.

Like other negative emotions, anger seems to create an increase in attention—a *cognitive* response—toward things in the environment that provoke the anger (e.g., Eckhardt & Cohen, 1997; Cohen, Eckhardt, & Schagat, 1998). When people are really angry, they just seem to notice more things in the environment to be ticked off about. In a good mood, the guy going slow in the fast lane isn't a big deal. When you're filled with anger, it feels like a felony—even if you aren't in the fast lane yourself! This drain on the cognitive capacity may be a reason many angry people can't seem to think of anything but what they are angry at. This makes it hard for them to come up with other ways of thinking about the situation or to use coping responses. When we get heated up by some infraction, it always seems worse in terms of injustice, violation, and deliberate provocation in the heat of the moment than it does after we've cooled down.

So, when the anger mechanism is activated, emotional, physical and cognitive changes occur quite rapidly. An uncomfortable, swelling emotion coupled with tension and restless energy, like the body is winding up, plus a complete cognitive investment in the event that has been deemed unfair, and an exaggeration of the unfairness, all combine to make one *behavioral* response more likely: fight.

Anger, Inside and Out

Like anxiety, anger has a behavioral goal that is very necessary for survival. Indeed, without anger we would not have survived as a species. We'd be living under the rocks with the pill bugs and the skinks. There have been, and will always be, situations in which "fight" instead of "flight" is the most adaptive response. Situations involving protection of children, acquisition of mates, defense of territory, self-defense, and breaking free from bondage are examples. Though anger in and of itself is often considered something bad in its own right, many modern situations continue to require an anger-based response. Assertiveness, competition, discipline, and protection are a few examples.

However, some people have anger management problems. When most people think of an anger problem, they think of some hothead in the pool hall playing "Cue Ball Bat" with people's torsos. Actually there are two kinds of anger problems. The hothead in the pool hall might qualify as possessing an *externalizing anger problem*. He heats up too often, his anger is too intense, and he fights too much. He vents his anger outside of himself; that is, he externalizes. The other type of anger problem, which is more common to depressed people, is an *internalizing anger problem*. Here, events occur which would lead to anger and assertive behavior in most people, but in these people, for some reason, the anger is turned inside, or internalized. It is stuffed down, denied, or mishandled instead of expressed directly.

Let's consider the difference between an externalizing and internalizing anger problem, breaking a scenario down into its cognitive, emotional, and behavioral parts. Consider June, who is angry at her husband, Don, for forgetting their wedding anniversary.

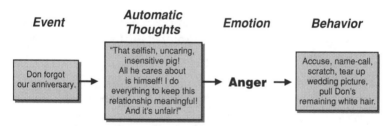

For the person who externalizes anger, the cognitive-behavioral target symptoms would be the exaggerated and black or white automatic thoughts and the overly aggressive, impulsive behavioral responses to anger.

The internalizing anger problem is more complex. Let's look at June again, up until the time she experiences anger. In this case, there are three potential emotional responses to anger.

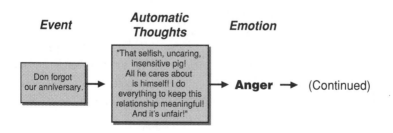

The first continuation leaves June hiding her anger deep inside:

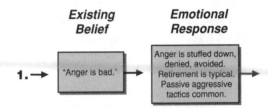

Existing Belief   **Emotional Response**

1. → "Anger is bad." → Anger is stuffed down, denied, avoided. Retirement is typical. Passive aggressive tactics common. →

Here, a strong belief that anger is not acceptable keeps June from expressing her anger with outward behavior. So anger just dams up, or is expressed in a passive implicit manner. An example of passive aggressive behavior might be for June to deliberately burn Don's breakfast. "Oops, I'm sorry, Don," she might say. "And to think those were the last two eggs."

The next continuation is common to depression, in which anger is morphed into a completely different, and more uncomfortable, negative emotion:

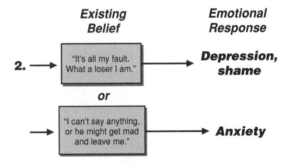

Existing Belief   **Emotional Response**

2. → "It's all my fault. What a loser I am." → **Depression, shame**

or

→ "I can't say anything, or he might get mad and leave me." → **Anxiety**

Here, automatic thoughts lead to depression or anxiety because of a new conceptualization of the event. First she's angry, now she's depressed, simply because she came up with different thoughts about the event that made her angry.

Why would this happen? Anger is a powerful, primal response that compels us to vindicate, or to take back what was unjustly swiped. Many people seem to block the expression of anger. Often, this tendency has a develop-

**Internalized anger: Those who know Melanie
believe that she never gets angry.**

mental cause; that is, when the person who internalizes
anger was a child, anger management was not modeled correctly or managed appropriately in the home.

In many families anger isn't expressed at all, or, more
commonly, it is invalidated. "If you're a good boy, we'll go
to the zoo today," says Dad, for example. So, little Joey cleans
his room and obeys every command. "When are we going to
the zoo, Dad?" Joey asks. To which Pop replies, "Never! I'm
busy with this project. And don't give me any backtalk,
either. You get plenty of goodies." If this sort of event occurs
aplenty in a person's formative years, it can lead to a knee-
jerk tendency to twist anger into shame or depression.

Some people are taught to fear anger. Violent households
often breed this sort of thing. There are folks that are downright phobic of anger and will do anything to avoid any conflict that might activate it. They feel as if anger will cause
them to suddenly burst into flames.

Some people go back and forth between anger and depression or anxiety and anger, and so on. This would qualify as a blend of externalizing and internalizing anger. Often individuals who self-mutilate, or who make suicidal gestures that have a motive other than wanting to die (for example, if a woman overdoses after a fight with her boyfriend, then immediately tells her boyfriend she has done so, for the purpose of "showing him" how much he's hurt her), are often trapped in this roller coaster of rage and shame. That leads to the third continuation:

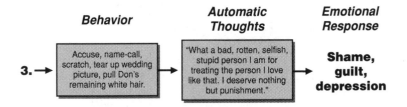

Behavior	**Automatic Thoughts**	**Emotional Response**
3. → Accuse, name-call, scratch, tear up wedding picture, pull Don's remaining white hair.	→ "What a bad, rotten, selfish, stupid person I am for treating the person I love like that. I deserve nothing but punishment."	→ **Shame, guilt, depression**

One way of looking at appropriate anger management is in terms of balance renewal. Anger is experienced when an imbalance occurs in terms of what the individual reckons as fair or equitable. If anger-driven action promotes the return to balance, anger is resolved and goes away. Here's an example of a reply that balances the situation and defuses the anger.

Situation: Ron made an elaborate dinner for Denny. She is late and didn't call. Dinner is cold. Ron is very angry.

Ron: "I'm angry you didn't call and let me know you were going to be late. The meal is cold."

Denny: "You're right. I was totally wrapped up in my conversation with Rosa. I'm sorry. Can I help salvage it?"

Result: Ron is no longer mad. They heat up the chicken casserole and have a nice evening.

With the externalizing anger problem, even though the imbalance may have occurred because of an unjust behavior, extreme responses don't return the situation to balance; rather, they just shift the imbalance in the other direction. In other words, the aggressive methods of the person who is externalizing his anger result in extreme and unjust actions toward others, who in turn are left in a state of imbalance. With the internalizing anger problem, the imbalance caused by inequity does not change, as the individual cannot—because of rigid beliefs or automatic thoughts that turn anger to potentially crippling emotions like depression, shame, or anxiety—permit actions that would lead to a return to balance.

Quelling the Noisiest of Moods

As we've already said, managing both externalizing and internalizing anger problems requires breaking down the experience and identifying the changeable cognitive and behavioral parts. For many people, the most important key to help them change is learning to instill a sense of control over anger. Though the internalizing anger problem will also require the identification and control of thoughts that block anger or change anger into other negative emotions, I've found that helping people feel more in control of their anger, as a first step, is always helpful regardless whether it is over-expressed or internalized.

To this day, you sometimes read that the way to cure stuffed down or unexpressed anger is to just get angry more, to let it out, to vent. Once, hospitalized teens with such problems were allowed to whack each other with "harmless" foam clubs called Bahtakas. The theory behind this was that this "expression of anger" somehow released the pent up rage, as though it were some sort of gas or accumulating pus. There is no such hydraulic system of mind, and just "expressing anger" does not always reduce it; indeed, it can heat someone up all the more. Further, as we've said before, many people with internalizing anger problems fear angry arousal, or they have legitimate experiences where their anger has gotten out of control. Having confidence that he can bring a state of high anger or rage down to a moderate or mild level is an essential skill for the externalizer or internalizer.

Eva Feindler and her colleagues (e.g., Feindler & Ecton, 1988; Feindler, 1991), who have published a great deal on the topic of adolescent anger and cognitive therapy, contend that in order to control anger, it must be slowed down. When depression creeps in, it has an insidious onset with many opportunities to intervene and counter symptoms before a full-blown episode of depression occurs. Anger, on the other hand, has a rapid onset. A person can literally go from a sedate condition to utter rage in a matter of seconds. Though anger can come on quickly, there are opportunities to catch symptoms and reduce the state. Like depression, it is best to catch the symptoms early on, before you are steeped in the negative emotion.

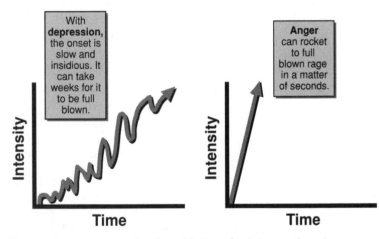

Depression comes on slowly, with time for intervention. Anger can burst onto the scene all at once, with little time for intervention.

Help for the Externalizer

People with externalizing anger problems think about things differently than do people who don't have this problem. Let's look at some of those cognitive factors, or ways of thinking, and look at suggestions for using cognitive tools to control anger. Most of the research from which these notions stem was done with aggressive adolescents.

1. *Interpreting events as provoking when they are not, then jumping to inaccurate, hostile conclusions.* Based on the work of Raymond Novaco, Ph.D. (1979), John Lochman, Ph.D. (1984) and others, it is clear that people with anger control problems, when provoked, do not sufficiently process the event; rather, they jump quickly to hostile conclusions. People with anger control problems often misconstrue events in such a way that they feel deliberately provoked even when they are not. With depression, the misconstructions are of the hopelessness, helplessness and worthlessness sort; with anger, the themes are unfairness, violation, injustice, deliberate provocation and the like.

In states of tremendous rage, it is best to remove yourself from the anger-provoking situation. As with panic, when one is consumed with rage, there is very little one can do to counter distorted thoughts. Get away and cool down a bit. Then, when you can think straight, set yourself into "metacognitive overdrive."

To counter anger's tunnel vision, ask yourself if there is another way of looking at the event. Try to entertain one or two other non-malicious explanations for what you've interpreted as unfairness, violation or deliberate provocation. Often this is enough to at least decrease anger to the level of mild frustration. For example, let's say the driver in front of you is going too slowly. You might think, "He's an idiot." Or, you might try thinking, "He is old and cautious, or maybe he's lost; maybe he lost someone to an automobile accident and is really careful on the road now."

A test of evidence can be an effective way to discover exaggerations in our thinking when angry. However, the thought record does not lend itself to most angry encounters, which come on quickly. If you've identified a thought like, "He's trying to annoy me," simply ask yourself two questions: "Where is the evidence?" and "Is there any evidence that refutes this conclusion?" Sometimes all it takes is one bit of refuting data to bring anger down to a manageable level.

2. *Difficulty taking another's perspective*. Little and Kendall (1979), as well as other researchers in the area of anger control, found that non-aggressive adolescents are better than aggressive adolescents at shifting out of anger's tunnel vision and evaluating other people's perspectives. Deficiencies in the skill of perspective-taking would certainly make a person more prone to having frequent and prolonged episodes of anger.

If you are having an angry conflict with someone, put yourself in their shoes. Try to see things from their perspective. Really attempt to show that you are trying to understand their concerns. Avoid accusations. Use "I" statements to express your feelings, such as "I feel angry when you interrupt me," or "I don't like it when you make plans before talking with me." Avoid "you" messages, such as "You self-centered hog; you never consider what I want when you make plans." When you are angry about "non-human" events, try to understand their occurrence from a standpoint other than injustice. For example, "The traffic is really bad on the freeway this Saturday . . . but maybe it's because there are a lot of people who have stressful jobs like me and like to get away on the weekends." In many relationships, the things that anger us have angered us for decades, and they haven't changed a bit. Often, they are relatively small in the grand scheme of things. Ask yourself, "Is this really a big deal? Can I live with it?"

Raymond DiGuiseppe, Ph.D., (1999) has been interested in the application of a kind of cognitive therapy called Rational Emotive Therapy to anger problems. He sees many angry people shaking their "shoulds" like a holy book. "My mother-in-law should treat me nicer," or "My husband should clean up after himself," or "My friend should be less of a cheapskate." DiGuiseppe asserts that "shoulds" do nothing but keep us miserable, and usually, though we uphold them as laws etched in stone, they don't fit with the facts at all. Using the example of a cheapskate friend, perhaps I am angry and say to myself regularly, "He should change! He should change!" even though he's been a cheap-skate for the 10 years I've known him. Why should he change? A better belief would be, "He probably won't change" coupled with "I would like it if he changed." This may sound like nothing but word play, but there is a con-siderable difference between "should" and "want." "Should" means he has to stop being a cheapskate, and if he doesn't he's breaking my law. "Want" doesn't require that he change at all; it merely hopes he does. If I want him to change, and he doesn't, no laws have been broken. Further, using "want" puts me in a position to simply cope with this unchanging tendency by not letting it get to me and by not putting myself in situations in which I feel cheated.

3. *Difficulty anticipating outcomes before action.* People with-out anger problems are able to control how they respond to anger and actually keep it from getting out of control by pre-dicting what could happen if they "lose it." For example, driving in a rugged part of the county and getting cut off by a gang of bikers with daggers and skull emblems on the backs of their jackets might lead to the urge to roll down the window and make a very rude gesture, but one doesn't typ-ically give into the urge, due to the prediction that such a gesture might lead to considerable harm.

Phillip Kendall and his colleagues (e.g., Little & Kendall, 1979) have focused on helping adolescents with anger prob-lems increase their ability to imagine and evaluate alterna-tives and to slow down impulsive action with self-talk. Peo-ple with anger problems tend to respond to provocation impulsively. Thinking of the potential outcomes of our actions is not easy, much less when we are in a state of extreme anger. Anger is myopic, and extreme anger almost always has negative consequences when channeled onto another person. If you are angry, there in the heat of the moment, try to visualize the future. Try to come up with several potential negative consequences to losing control of your anger. You might ask yourself questions such as "If I act hostile toward my boss right now, what will the outcome be in terms of future employment?" or "If I continue to fight with my wife, could this go on until 2 A.M.?"

Anger can flare up on you quite rapidly and before you know it, you're consumed with it. Learn to recognize the early symptoms of anger. For most people, the early symptoms are physical and may include tensing of the jaw, restlessness, or a flushed face. Many people don't recognize these early warning signs, and consequently keep escalating. Feindler advocates the use of verbal cues, like "Cool it!" or "Anger alert!" or "Stop!" Regular pairing of anger's physical symptoms with a verbal cue can actually fuse them to the point that when the symptoms come on, the word just pops into mind. Furthermore, try to relax. Pay attention to your body's reaction as you get angry. You may be breathing harder and faster or have an adrenaline rush, a headache, stomach pain, tension in the neck, clenched fists, or tightness in the chest. The same relaxation techniques for managing anxiety (such as muscle relaxation, diaphragmatic breathing, and distraction) can be very effective for controlling anger. You cannot be relaxed and full of rage at the same time!

Aggression, verbal or otherwise, occurs because the crime just seems too huge; it must be vindicated now. Often in life, the injustices we encounter turn out to be less of a big deal an hour or so later. Too often, we don't realize this until it's too late—when you're sleeping on the couch or sitting in a cell. We all can recall a time when we've expressed anger righteously, then two hours later felt guilty for the things we've said. At the time those actions felt appropriate, but later, when the anger has fizzled out, they seem out of line. Two words can make all the difference if you allow yourself to really dwell on them: *So what?* Isn't there a beautiful ring to it? So what? So the guy changed lanes without signaling. *So what?* Does this infraction really amount to anything given the day ahead of you? Will you even remember it two hours from now?

Help for the Internalizer

Controlling anger does not mean stuffing it down or denying it. Rather, it means keeping it at a level that is on par with the violation and not avoiding it, while at the same time not blowing up.

Why do so many depressed people internalize anger? It's more accurate to ask, "Why do so many people who internalize anger get depressed?" Remember, anger has been with us for a long time. Indeed, you would be hard pressed to find a member of the animal kingdom that doesn't seem to have some sort of anger response stowed in its brain, even if its brain is the size of a little walnut.

Anger is supposed to occur in threat situations where we perceive violation, injustice, unfairness, or deliberate provocation, and where the possible consequences are too high to simply give up or run away. Here's what's supposed to happen: 1. Someone wrongs me. 2. I get angry. 3. I do something about it to right the wrong. 4. If successful, I feel better. 5. In response to such a sequence, my brain says, "Good boy. You are powerful," and I go on my merry way.

When people are rendered powerless or defeated in life, they often become depressed. Preventing anger from driving some sort of forceful action renders an individual powerless too. Think about it. If an injustice occurs to someone and he internalizes his anger, he is in essence backing away. Injustice prevails. Depression may occur even though no battle was actually fought and lost. People who allow themselves to be walked on regularly, even if they could have been victorious over these walkers, often get depressed simply because of a poverty of victories in the face of injustice.

Depressed people who internalize anger need to begin bringing about some victories. They need to allow anger to be expressed appropriately and to drive successful assertive action. Time and time again, I've listened to previously depressed people who internalize anger say that they have experienced mood improvement as they began to spread their wings in their relationships and express their needs, object to infractions, express their dissatisfaction when inappropriate behavior occurs, and move away from situations in which they are belittled, put down, or marginalized.

Unblocking Internalized Anger

People block and internalize anger for a variety of reasons, most of which are cognitive, that is, having to do with catastrophic predictions or self-debasing assumptions that anger is bad or sinful. Here are a few: "I don't deserve to have my needs met," "Anger is wrong; if I express it, I'm a bad person, especially if I express it toward someone I love," "I will hurt others," "I'll be overpowered if I get angry," and "I'll be abandoned if I get angry."

If someone has wronged you and you find yourself steeped in shame and guilt, or you are angry but feel unable to do something about it, ask yourself "What would be the negative consequences of acting assertively about this injustice?" Often you'll come up with answers such as "I'll just feel worse because they'll put me down even more," or "My friend might never speak to me again," or "I won't be able to control my anger. I'll do irreparable harm." Another question to ask yourself is "What would expressing my anger right now say about me?" Often, you'll come up with such self-statements as "I'm selfish," or "I am ungrateful for the things my wife has done for me," or "I deserve punishment."

Now you have a Big Bad Thought, and are in a position to use any of the many disputation strategies presented in previous chapters. For example, if "I'm selfish" is identified, a good comeback would be "What would I say to someone I care about if they had been mistreated and were thinking it would be selfish to express dissatisfaction with this treatment?" Or, if "I'm deserving of punishment" was the negative thought, a test of evidence would be in order, including the Dr. Frankenstein technique in which you would build a monster definitely deserving of punishment then compare yourself to it. To the idea of "I'll be overpowered," fight back with a reminder of past situations in which you have expressed yourself assertively and have not been overpowered; or, in line with the cognitive exposure strategy for anxiety management, remind yourself of all available options if you were, in fact, overpowered. For example, you might say, "I could stay in there and continue asserting myself instead of walking away like some overridden loser," or "I could end the discussion, not defeated, but with a conclusion in which we agree to disagree, then walk away neither victor nor loser."

Assertiveness: Pros and Caveats

It is beyond the scope of this book to thoroughly address assertiveness training. There are a variety of very good books on assertiveness that address both the behavioral and communication skills necessary, as well as the cognitive obstacles to appropriate assertive action. Remember, assertiveness is not the same as aggressiveness. The cognitive strategies we've looked at for bringing high anger and rage down should be a part of any assertiveness package. You can't act assertively if you have smoke billowing out of your ears. You have to cool down first and get to a point in which you can reason, a point in which your veins aren't bulging on your neck and brow and your fists aren't throbbing like two big lungs.

Some components of effective assertiveness:

1. *Body language.* Envision the sort of stance, facial expression, and mannerisms you are more likely to respond to when someone is attempting to be assertive or is making a request for a change in your behavior. Do you respond to someone who is talking thunderously, rolling their eyes, shaking their head, hissing, sneering, sighing, or arching back with fists clenched? Didn't think so. Assertiveness should be rendered from a relaxed but appropriately postured body. There should be evidence of concern and dissatisfaction on the face, but not disgust and rage. These are sure-fire ways to get into a fight, and prob-

ably lose. "Cool, calm and collected" is much less likely to set someone off.

2. *Empathy.* Before you take someone on for an infraction, sit down for a few minutes and think about her position. What are some non-malevolent reasons she did what she did? Might you have done the same thing, or something like it, if you were in her shoes? If you go into a conflict with the belief that the other's behavior was unimaginable and unforgivable, you are not likely to be successfully assertive. Further, express empathy in your delivery. The statement "Jack, you are an insensitive worm for not calling," will be less likely to increase Jack's tendency to phone in than the statement "Jack, I totally know what it's like to be swamped at work; I've been there myself. I'd sure like it if you'd phone in the afternoon to let me know if you're going to be late."

3. *Keep it brief.* Some people, when angry about the behavior of another, feel it is time to regurgitate every past inequity, as though to do so will make a better case for what they are currently angry about. All this does is make people more defensive. Keep the assertive conversation limited to the problem at hand. Also, don't lecture. No one likes to be criminalized with some half-hour Grand Jury indictment.

4. *Accept some things.* It would be nice if we got everything we wanted and people always only did things that we approve of. Sorry, wrong planet. Some of the things that continue to bother us have bothered us for years. Are they really ever likely to change? If not, would a better course of action be for you to learn how to live with them? Of course, I'm not advocating that you put up with being victimized or constantly put down. I'm referring here to relationships in which there are inherent differences in partners; for example, one is a slob, the other is compulsive cleaner. Neither is likely to change completely to suit the other's extreme. Some degree of acceptance in

both parties, it would seem, would be vital for this relationship's happy endurance.

5. *Use "I" statements.* For Rick to come barreling into the kitchen saying, "You really ticked me off today, Susan!" is to provoke a shouting match. "Susan, I'm feeling angry about how this day is going," is much more likely to make Sue willing to listen, because Sue is not being immediately blamed for the anger. It's Rick's anger.

6. *Consider compromise.* Rarely do people enjoy being told what to do; some, indeed, despise even being asked respectfully to do something. For the one initiating assertiveness to suggest a compromise when an impasse is reached is a powerful way of deescalating a rising conflict, and also getting at least some of what she is requesting.

7. *Don't whine or nag.* An assertive tone comes without the excess emotional baggage. To whine and nag is infantile and infantilizing. Try to keep your tone stable. This does not mean you should drone on in a completely flat manner with eyes at half-mast, which can convey a complete indifference to the other's point of view. Instead, try to speak in a way that, if the tables were turned, you would consider authentic and not patronizing.

8. *Don't expect assertiveness to always pan out swimmingly.* I've read a few self-help books in which the authors herald assertiveness as the magic key to conflict resolution, implying that it is all you need for healthy interpersonal functioning.

This is a set-up for disappointment. Just because you are appropriate in your spoken complaint or request for change doesn't mean the recipient is going to mirror this. In fact, you could earn a top award for assertiveness and still get nothing more than "Get the heck out of my room!" from the recipient of your assertiveness.

Choose your battles carefully—and know when to walk away from one in which there is no way a peaceful resolution will be reached. Intense interpersonal conflict is very taxing, and it should be avoided if possible. This may sound contradictory to the previous call for increased assertiveness, but remember, conflict is a part of life. When it comes your way, or when you must initiate it because you are the recipient of some inequity, assertiveness can increase your sense of power and control. But again, be wise with regard to battles selected. Ask yourself, "Is there a strong possibility that attempting assertiveness with this person will do nothing but make me feel more miserable?" If the answer is yes, it might be worthwhile to keep some distance from the unswerving annoyance and put your energies elsewhere. Assertiveness is not a panacea. Like all of the strategies presented in this book, it is likely to help in some circumstances, not all.

Main Points

1. Some depressed people have problems with anger as well. Anger has emotional, physical, cognitive, and behavioral symptoms. Anger causes people to focus on whatever is causing the anger. Anger also blocks memories and beliefs that might prevent aggressive or assertive action. Angry people tend to exaggerate the unfairness and injustice of events. The basic purpose of anger is to drive the fight response. Indeed, there are some situations in which anger is very necessary for survival. Without anger, we would simply flee from every threat situation.

2. There are two types of anger problems: *externalizing,* in which there is too much intense anger and aggressive behavior, and *internalizing,* in which injustice and violations are occurring, but the person doesn't allow himself to have angry expression or take any assertive

action. Internalizing anger problems are common with depressed people.

3. For both people who externalize anger and people who internalize anger, it is important to develop some control over anger arousal. Anger control does not mean stuffing down anger. It entails catching angry arousal early on, and moderating it so that the behavioral response is equal with the "crime" at hand. There is little one can do when consumed with rage except get away from the provoking situation. Many of the cognitive strategies helpful with depression can be applied to anger, too. They involve reducing the perceived injustice, empathizing with the other person or the situation causing the anger, considering consequences, and testing angry thoughts for evidence.

4. It is not helpful for people who internalize anger to simply "get angry" more. Many people who internalize anger have concerns that anger will get out of control or cause some irreparable harm. It is helpful for those people to challenge catastrophic predictions of anger expression and self-debasing labels, and to practice anger control strategies as they begin to allow anger to drive assertive action.

5. Assertiveness is a vital skill for both people who externalize anger and people who internalize anger. Unlike aggression, assertive communication involves respectfully and concisely articulating concerns, complaints, or requests in a manner that does not inflame others or provoke a fight. Body language, empathy, and brevity of speech are important components of assertiveness, as are acceptance, the use of "I" statements, compromise, and tone of voice.

Chapter Ten:

Relapse Prevention I: Nipping Melancholy Buds

My primary goal in writing this book was to help people extract themselves from depression. Depression is a terrible experience to endure, and many people's depressions go untreated. Consequently, people who might respond wonderfully to an antidepressant medication and/or cognitive therapy sometimes endure months of gloom. Getting out of depression involves preventing the symptoms from perpetuating the state.

Eliminating a depression is an arduous job; relief comes in a patchy manner, and bringing about even tiny patches can be exhausting. Depression does break though, and when it does, man, oh, man, it's like living in a black and white TV for a month, and then waking up one day inside one of those 36-inch, digital color beauties.

Ogre in the midst: Use your new cognitive tools to keep the ogre on the outside.

It is equally important to keep depression away. There's nothing worse than working your rear end off on something for weeks only to have the whole thing collapse in your lap. Recuperation after depression can be like that. You've whacked the depressive ogre clean off your chest and you feel great, only to wake up one gray morning to discover that foul ogre peering in your bedroom window with a sick, maniacal grin on his greasy face.

A relapse of depression is serious. One of the strongest predictors of having an episode of depression is having suffered a previous episode (Garber & Flynn, 2001). I'm not saying you should start trembling and dreading the return of depression, because it's not necessarily true that you will experience another bout, but you need to be mindful of the potential for the ogre's revisit, and not ignore subtle symptoms if they start creeping in. When it comes to depression, there's a significant difference between a lapse and a relapse. It's not like some views of alcohol dependence, in which one rum cookie after six months of sobriety equates to a relapse. A lapse, as opposed to a relapse, is non-severe; that is, it involves a return of some of the symptoms of the depression, not all of them. Plus, a lapse is mild to moderate in terms of intensity. A relapse, on the other hand, involves a full-blown return of the symptoms of the depression. A lapse doesn't last, where as a relapse endures for a long time. Lastly, a lapse is something someone can usually rebound from on his or her own, whereas a relapse often requires the help of a professional.

Lapse	**Relapse**
• Non-severe	• Severe
• Short term	• Prolonged
• Rarely requires professional intervention	• Usually requires professional help

There's a lot you can do to turn a lapse into a relapse. Let's say you've been feeling fit and functional for a week after suffering a month of depression. Then, for some reason you wake up on Monday and don't feel right. It's not full-blown depression, but you know it's something like depression. It's a heavy, sad woe and dread, a tide of tearfulness welling up, a lack of energy, a pull to stay in bed. And you say to yourself, "Oh, crud; I'm depressed again," which isn't true, as the experience is about one quarter the intensity of the depression you've just come out of. But you convince yourself that you are in fact, depressed again. You shrink into a fetal ball and decide to stay in bed all day. All the while, as you drift in and out of defeated half sleep, you're thinking, "This cognitive stuff was nonsense. I'm forever doomed to feel bad," and "What's the use? Forget it." The gloom worsens, and you're back to entertaining the negative threesome of hopelessness, helplessness, and worthlessness. Come day three of this, lo and behold, the cruel ogre's right back on your chest, plus he's invited his ugly friend Anxiety and his sadomasochistic girlfriend, Shame, to come on over and crash on your chest too.

This little relapse anecdote is akin to what Dr. G. Alan Marlatt, an internationally known expert in the area of addictive behavior, terms the Abstinence Violation Effect (Marlatt, 1978). According to Marlatt, many individuals actually turn a lapse into a relapse by virtue of their punitive self-statements and "forget it" attitude following a lapse.

Let's look at Jennifer, a recovering heavy drinker who has been on the wagon for a month before she goes to a stressful family wedding. She gets into an altercation with her obnoxious Uncle Don, who's been downing glass after glass of champagne. Unable to deal with it, Jennifer barrels over to the drink station, sucks down half a glass, then stops. Guilt seeps upward from her gut and she says, "Crud. I relapsed. I messed up. I violated my code of abstinence. They are all going to yell at me at the alcohol abuse prevention meeting the day after tomorrow when I confess. Oh, to heck with it."

I guess I'm just an alcoholic!" So what does Jennifer do? Of course, she finishes the glass and requests another.

It's been important in cognitive therapy to help recovering patients challenge distorted assumptions and beliefs about mild to moderate dips in mood, such as "If I feel low again, I've failed," or "Any dip in mood means clinical depression again," or "If I have a bad day that affects my mood, I'm back where I started." Such beliefs actually turn lapses into relapses because they create a mindset of defeat and help-lessness which worsens mood, and also makes it likely the person will allow behaviors that worsen mood further.

Relapse prevention is not about preventing lapses. It is about keeping lapses from becoming full-blown relapses. To do this, there are five things you need to do: expect and not catastrophize lapses; know your early warning signs; know your primary triggers and prepare for them; and continue to use cognitive tools. We'll look at each of these points in more detail next.

Expect Lapses

Remember, you will probably have some lapses. Don't fear them! They're normal, to be expected. Depression is a nasty, thick, viscous stuff that doesn't just wipe off. It breaks, and when it does, you know you're not depressed anymore, but the system has been shaken up considerably. There will be some days when you feel like it's trying to pull you back down. As explained before, depression involves a strong activation of certain information processing networks. After the depression is deactivated, it doesn't take as much to reactivate it. It may be that there are some biochemical vestiges lingering for a while. At any rate, you are going to be a little fragile, a little more emotionally reactive, and a little less resilient when a crummy day squeezes into the week.

Don't catastrophize a lapse. Some people find that after they've broken from the depression, they still have that heavy gloom in the morning. This is almost certainly bio-chemical. Don't freak out about it. Get up. Get moving. The more you see that not giving into the dips results in mood improvement, the more you'll accept the morning dips as no big deal. I often liken it to my arthritis; sometimes I wake up with extra stiffness and pain, and I need to get up and move around, or it's pain and stiffness all day.

If you have a lapse, try to look at it as an opportunity to learn, as opposed to a failure, or as something terrible. When people are trying to change an addictive behavior, the lapses, the temptations, and the urges are all opportunities to rebound quicker and configure their lives so that the triggers aren't so prevalent. The same holds true with depression. So you got in an argument with your spouse and you're feeling glum. This is a perfect opportunity to do a Thought Record Flow Sheet or the Thought Debate, or to practice a more assertive response. A lapse successfully quelled could be looked at as being even more powerful in terms of relapse prevention than having a period of no lapses at all.

Know the Early Warning Signs

Having been through an episode of depression, you are now in a position to look back objectively and pinpoint the early symptoms of the onset of depression. Depression is insidious; it comes on gradually, like some rising bog. People vary with regard to which symptoms emerge first. Though depression is a mood disorder, sad mood is not always the first symptom to occur. For some people, the initial symptoms are physical. A very common early warning sign is insomnia, or any disruption in the normal sleep pattern. You may recall that in the time leading up to your full blown depression, you regularly woke up in the wee hours, worrying and worrying, unable to get back to sleep. Conversely, many people slipping into depression will sleep

more, finding themselves sleeping in later and later whenever they can get away with it. People often complain of
having no energy or drive, and just wanting to lie around
and do nothing. Changes in appetite often occur early when
depression is setting in. Losing weight when you are not
attempting or desiring to do so can be a clue that something
is wrong. On the other hand, eating more, not out of hunger,
but for the purpose of relieving boredom or negative emotions, can be a red flag.

The reoccurrence of a few physical symptoms like those
of depression doesn't necessarily mean you are becoming
depressed again. But if they seem to be enduring, or worsening, it would be a good idea to err on the side of relapse
prevention as opposed to just sticking them out. If you are
taking a medication, you should notify your doctor. It may
be that a modification in your medication is necessary. Don't
postpone making an appointment with your doctor if you
think you might be getting depressed again. Remember, it is
easier to pull out of depression early on than it is when
you're entrenched and incapacitated. If you are not currently taking medication, and you find the depression creeping back, it might be time to give an antidepressant a try.

For some people, the early warning signs are behavioral.
You may find yourself slowly regressing back into withdrawal, declining invitations to do things with your pals, not
leaving the house, or not attending to your appearance. Or
you may find that you are not doing things that previously
brought you pleasure. Maybe you are canceling workouts, are
not reading, or are not engaging in hobbies. Or maybe things
aren't getting done. The house is neglected, with dishes
piled up in the sink and a layer of crud on all the counters.
Ask yourself, "What's going on?" Do an inventory of current
life stressors. Is there a conflict going on right now that needs
closure or a different approach? Do you need some help
with some burden that feels impossible? Address these problems now, before this depression seizes you entirely again.

It's easy to slip back into behaviors that go along with depression; therefore, it is recommended that you continue to use some sort of activity schedule every day. You may think that now that you're feeling better, you don't need to fill out a schedule every day, but believe me, if you wake up with depressive tar all over yourself and your bed, it will be it will be easier to stay on course if you have plans than it will be if you've left the day completely open.

Still other people will recall cognitive symptoms as being the most noticeable early on in their depression; they may notice concentration problems, confusion, memory deficits, or the presence of negative thoughts, particularly self-critical ones. An inordinate amount of worry and self-focused attention is often a call that something isn't right. Don't forget about the cognitive tools we've talked about. You may find that you are doing fine without sitting down and doing a Thought Record Flow Sheet, but again, if you find your mood sinking, and the cinderblock attached to your mood seems to be a Big Bad Thought, sit down and do a thought record or any of the other disputation strategies you've learned here.

It has been established that the belief that one has social support available can prove to be a buffer to depression (e.g., Cohen & Willis, 1985; Lepore, 1992). If you feel like you're slipping, call on a friend or family member you trust. Some folks who've come out of depression worry that since they've "put their friends and family through so much," they had better keep it to themselves next time. A good remedy for this concern is to give your friends and family a "heads up" that you may need a little extra of their time while you're coming out of this bad patch. You might say something on the lines of, "Jack, I'm feeling a lot better, and I think this depression is flushed for good. You've been a real pal through all this, and I'm indebted to you. I hope it ain't a burden, but I may need to call you now and then, for a little booster shot from this fine friendship."

Know Your Primary Triggers and Prepare for Them

People vary when it comes to depression triggers. What sends one person into depression might have minimal emotional impact on another. Think back. Then think forward. Anything upcoming that resembles what set off your depression last time? If so, you need to prepare for it. Very often in the outpatient cognitive therapy program, people have left feeling better, but have also left in the direction of the very life stressors that brought them to therapy: a divorce with bitterness still in the brew; a termination from a job that is a reality; a return to a job that was at the onset of the depression fraught with discord. The ones who do well usually have a different game plan for how these stressors will be dealt with.

There are three things you need to ask yourself: 1. Are there any potential triggers on the horizon? 2. Are they avoidable? 3. If not, how will I deal with them differently, so I don't get depressed again? Just because the stressors might be avoidable doesn't mean avoidance is always the best call. Avoiding your caustic mother-in-law for a while might be an appropriate limitation, but leaving your 12-year career might not be. I think it is a good idea to keep some distance from things strongly associated with depression for a while if you can. Certain people, parts of town, even certain driving routes, can have the power to evoke the negative emotions just by virtue of their past association. There are props out there that have depression spilled all over them.

I recall a woman whose room became a dark, dank cave when she was depressed, with a huge rock door at the mouth of it and all. When she came out of the depression, she loathed the cave room and couldn't stand the way light fell on the walls, the smell of it, or the configuration of the fixtures. So she changed some things around and put up a new print, and also she used the room just for sleeping for a while. She couldn't get out of there quickly enough in the morning. As her positive mood continued to strengthen, the room lost its association with depression, and it became more inviting again.

**Leaving the dark cave of depression is the first step.
Then comes staying out.**

The stressors that aren't avoidable should be addressed now. Kids having behavioral or academic problems? Get some help from a counselor or a tutor. Marital problems? Consider the time right to get some therapy, or at least have a sit-down with your spouse to talk seriously about change. Miserable job? Problem-solve with your boss about a modification of duties. To stay in a defeated state or enter back into a defeated state when you are coming out of depression is like apologizing to the ogre and inviting him back inside for a chest rest.

If you are returning to an unchanged environment, try to remind yourself that you are not the same person you were before the depression. I recall June so well. She reported working for a boss who was a narrow-minded rage monger who had a mission statement written across her brain reminding her of her purpose in life, which was to belittle, put down, and generally have a tyrannical relationship with all her subordinates. June talked a lot about just leaving the job and finding another one. She was ready to march into her boss' office, give her a piece of her mind, then quit for good, perhaps knocking over a telephone or paperweight on her way out. That was certainly an option for June. However, she'd been with the company for 20 years and was one year from retiring. To outright quit would be to kiss bye-bye an excellent retirement package. So she decided to stick it out.

June took the attitude that even though the job hadn't changed, she had. She was more in control of her mood. Through her newfound metacognitive voice, she was less vulnerable to having a knee jerk anguish and shame response to her mean spirited boss.

Practice Cognitive Techniques Regularly

I recall taking two years of French in college. When the semester was over, I couldn't wait to sell my French book back to the bookstore. Done. Slowly all verb conjugations and phrases I'd memorized and regurgitated for quizzes and midterms faded to dust. And now I can't speak anything but a few words of it. I wish I'd kept it up. Like French, the cognitive skills can fade, too. Remember, in terms of evolution, metacognition is a pretty neonatal gift. If you stop practicing, it will fold back into fetal position and fall asleep.

Having a bad day? Something gnawing at you? Feeling glum and can't put your finger on why? Sit down and do identify the cognitive culprits, then dispute them to pieces. Or, if you're feeling rusty, review some of the techniques presented in this book.

I recall one creative patient in the outpatient program who was contacted some time after discharge. She said she had purchased a small dry erase marker board, then, with an indelible marker, had turned it into a permanent Thought Record Flow Sheet. When she felt bad, she'd pull it out, do the flow sheet with a dry marker, then erase it. She was enthusiastic about doing regular thought records, but didn't want to have to redo the form each time.

Remember, the ultimate goal of cognitive therapy is for people to be able to use metacognition at the drop of a hat and to be able to talk back to their automatic (or big bad) thoughts as though their brain has a new inhabitant who watches over things.

Feeling suddenly gloomy one morning, Julie later surprised her friend Ann by her ability to snap out of it with her new skills.

Following is a blank Relapse Prevention Worksheet. Personalize the material presented in this chapter, so you have it handy should one of those aforementioned dreary lapses occur.

Relapse Prevention Worksheet

What are possible early warning signs that I am becoming depressed again?

_____
_____
_____
_____

How will I catch these symptoms and prevent a lapse from becoming a full-blown relapse?

_____
_____
_____
_____

What are my primary triggers (high risk situations) for relapse?

_____
_____
_____
_____

Are these triggers avoidable? How? If not, how will I manage them differently, given what I've learned in the cognitive program?

_____
_____
_____
_____

Are there any high-risk situations coming up in the next month? Next year? How can I prepare myself for them, given what I've learned in the cognitive program?

_____
_____
_____
_____

6. Are there lifestyle or interpersonal buffers that I need to develop and/or implement to prevent relapse?

_____
_____
_____
_____

7. What cognitive therapy methods will I continue to use and practice to become more efficient at managing and preventing depression?

_____
_____
_____

Main Points

1. Getting out of depression is one thing, but staying out of it is another. With depression, there is a significant difference between a lapse and a relapse. A lapse is a brief reemergence of mild to moderate symptoms that many people can prevent from becoming a full-blown relapse. A relapse is a new, full-blown case of depression. Lapses are not failures, but opportunities to learn, and to become more and more able to understand your unique vulnerabilities.

2. It's easier to rebound from a lapse if you catch it early on. It is important to respond to early warning signs using cognitive resources or by seeking outside help. Early warning signs don't necessarily mean that depression is coming back, but for a few months after coming out of a depression, you are particularly vulnerable for relapse. The longer you can remain free of depression, the harder it is for depression to infiltrate and seize your life again.

3. Everyone is different in terms of relapse triggers. People recovering from depression need to take a proactive approach to relapse. Scan your future—especially the not-too-distant future—and ask yourself if there are any stressful or potentially disappointing events lurking out there that might have the power to pull you back down. It's important to know which potential triggers are avoidable, and if the triggers are not avoidable, know how you will manage them differently so they don't lead to relapse.

4. Cognitive therapy techniques work best when they're practiced. Even after you come out of depression it is important to do an occasional thought record, to continue reading about cognitive therapy, or perhaps see a cognitive therapist to do some longer-term core belief work. Like any skill, if you stop practicing, your abilities can start to decay. Being prepared means you don't give the depressive ogre the advantage he so malevolently desires.

Chapter Eleven:

Relapse Prevention II: Cutting Your Losses

A book devoted to helping people understand and combat depression would not be complete without some discussion of depression from an evolutionary perspective. Depression has been around for a long time. It exerts strong effects on our thinking, mood, motivation, and behavior. Could it be that the symptoms of depression have served some "purpose" in our ancient past?

This may seem like an absurd question, given how "unfit" we feel and behave when we're depressed, but keep in mind, the rules of survival are not always pretty. Check the rest of the animal kingdom. It can be downright ruthless out there. Survival is impossible without some degree of suffering. For some animals, survival equates to suffering. Recent research has offered a convincing model of depression in which the symptoms are said to have evolved because they served to demobilize—that is, to emotionally, physically, cognitively, and motivationally "shut down"—a defeated animal in a conflict situation.

A Defeat Strategy

Working from the ideas of British psychiatrist John Price in the 1960s and 1970s (e.g., Price, 1972), Paul Gilbert and his colleagues from the United Kingdom (1992, 2000) have pioneered an exciting new theory on the evolution of depression. The theory goes like this: For many mammals there are often conflicts over resources (e.g., food, nest sites and sexual opportunities). In conflict situations, an animal can't risk getting too injured (most conflicts are not fights to the death). In fact, most animals have basically two options: escalate (try to fight harder) or de-escalate (run away or give up).

How does an animal know when it is beaten and should give up? Although we don't know 'how' exactly, we do know that at some point those who are going to lose turn tail and run away or engage in submissive behaviors. Moreover, after a defeat, the losing animal goes though a period that looks similar to depression; the animal appears exhausted and is relatively passive, with elevated stress hormones.

Research by Gilbert's team has now shown that defeat has a special impact on positive mood; that is, defeat can sap joy and pleasure. If you think about this, it makes sense, because it means that defeated animals are unlikely to be full of confidence and looking forward to the future; rather they need to stay low and keep out of trouble. As Gilbert notes, a defeated animal must *keep* out of action until such time as it (and those around it) have accommodated to its defeat. If an animal simply had a good night's sleep and was back fighting or contesting again, there would be constant fighting, injuries would accumulate, and so forth.

Dino defeat. The flight mechanism prevented this defeated dino from further injury, but this response in humans can be triggered by non-life threatening conflicts, and the resulting feeling of defeat can lead to depression.

In essence, there seems to be an internal mechanism for de-escalation when it's clear that one has lost the fight; otherwise, animals (and people) would always just keep fighting to the death. That "mechanism" has to be compelling enough to make the organism back away, deflate, and to communicate "no threat" to its opponent. If the opponent cannot "see" it has won (e.g., the loser submits and hunkers down, avoids eye contact, and so on) then it might keep attacking. The mechanism must also be very uncomfortable emotionally; it must drive home cognitively that one is in an inferior position—weak, helpless, and subordinate. This mechanism must also make the body feel depleted and incapable of continued fight or struggling to succeed. Does this mechanism sound a lot like depression? Indeed.

Gilbert and his colleagues term this defeat response the Involuntary Defeat Strategy (IDS), and they maintain that the response is unique to humans only to the extent that the things that trigger it are often different from those that trigger the response in animals. The authors offer many non-human (even non-primate) examples of this very mechanism. Gilbert contends that the IDS doesn't have to lead to clinical depression. In fact, he claims that it usually doesn't. Conflicts occur, and the loser either successfully escapes or accommodates the defeat (e.g., the loser resolves the conflict or accepts a lower rank). Moreover, clinical depression is more likely if the loser identifies with the defeat response. Depression is an exaggeration of the IDS. It occurs when the IDS is activated and resolution cannot be achieved; that is, when the loser is clearly the loser, but he or she is blocked from escape or continues to remain embroiled in the conflict or struggle or can't reconcile to it. To use Gilbert's terminology, a depression that comes out of defeat is usually a function of either a "blocked escape" or an "arrested fight."

Every depressed person I've encountered whose depression was at least in part due to situational factors could sum up those factors as some sort of protracted defeat. Countless times, when someone was admitted to the hospital for depression, I've heard something to the effect that they just couldn't fight anymore. Examples include impossible jobs, getting fired unjustly, the dissolution of a relationship, over-whelming childrearing, losing a legal battle, being in a rela-tionship in which the person is belittled and cut down con-stantly by the partner, financial hardship, and failure to make friends or achieve intimacy.

The IDS is not just about fighting and defending to secure rank. It can also be triggered by failing to be deemed attrac-tive, worthy, desirable and so forth by others. If, for exam-ple, people have tried hard to make someone love them or to make their parents respect them, but no matter what they do, the other people just put them down, then they can per-ceive this as a heavy defeat and feel as if they are simply so low in worth that no one could value them. Another exam-ple is someone who has a weight problem and tells himself that "No one could value or respect me like this," and so places himself in a *low rank* position and sees others as if they are in some way better or superior to him. If that per-son tries hard to lose weight, but no matter how hard he struggles, he fails, then he can prolong this defeat mecha-nism, and, consequently, suffer depression.

Most people want to be respected, valued and included; it helps us feel good. Gaining rank is useful only to the extent that it gives access to resources, so it is the resources that are important to us. Humans seek to control the things that will lead to being respected, valued, and included. When we feel put down, devalued or undervalued, ex-cluded or rejected, we tend to feel bad because we get cut off from important resources, like the care, support, and help of others.

So it is not the case that everyone wants the top tier in terms of rank. Some like leadership and stardom, others don't. But most people will avoid very low rank because it could increase the risk of being bullied or not loved, etc. The belief that one is in control, has command of his or her life, is valued by others, and is tough enough not to be bullied and so forth is highly correlated with happiness and well-being.

However, being respected, valued, and included are not given for free (apart maybe from mother's love). People compete for those goals, be it in beauty contests or efforts to be a popular friend or lover. When we lose in the struggle to win respect and acceptance from other people, and from ourselves, we can feel inferior.

Now, as we saw above, it turns out that over millions of years some aspects of how our brains work have been evolving to cope with defeat, low rank, and put down. One way that animals, in the past, have coped with defeat is to be less positive and more anxious. This happens for humans, too. Think of how you feel when your favorite team loses or you put a lot of effort into something and fail. It may be true that having depression-like symptoms (reduced positive feelings and more negative feelings) in the face of defeat was actually an adaptive response in bygone days.

The IDS undoubtedly served us a long time ago by encouraging us to escape and de-escalate, as opposed to jumping back into the fray and risking death. Gilbert and his colleagues, however, make it clear that there is nothing "adaptive" about severe clinical depression, which, as stated, is often a problem with the operation of the IDS. If you worry about a defeat and tell yourself what a useless person you are, you are heaping attack on attack.

Most people experiencing situations like divorce, job loss, or rejection would experience depressive symptoms (or an activated IDS). Not all would become clinically depressed, however. Some would be able to get over the defeat, or move on and away from the defeat. Those who were blocked from escaping, refused to stop fighting, or who "cognitively" used the situation as evidence of "worthlessness" or "hopelessness" would be prone to an extended IDS activation, which is experienced as a profound depression.

Toward Hasty Defeats

In examining your lifestyle, it is important to ask yourself:

1. Am I in a prolonged defeat state—do I feel blocked and thwarted, or are there people in my life that put me down a lot?
2. Am I putting myself down so hard that I am beating myself up and making myself more defeated and depressed?
3. Am I fighting and fighting, when it's clear that the fight's over and I've lost?

If this sounds like your current situation, it is essential to consider another strategy that moves you out of protracted defeat.

Below are a variety of ways to diminish and make less likely a prolonged IDS, as well as the cognitive and behavioral strategies necessary in order to do so. We have looked at a variety of techniques for altering dysfunctional thinking and behaviors; however, some of the suggestions presented below will require additional help from a therapist trained and experienced in these areas.

Fight Harder

Sometimes, fighting harder is the appropriate strategy for an extended period of defeat. An example would be a passive, unassertive individual whose life is steeped in inequity, and who allows herself to be trampled on every day. Learning to effectively defend herself would decrease IDS activation.

Cognitive strategies: Use disputation and decatastrophizing strategies we have discussed earlier to reduce anxiety and uncertainty surrounding assertiveness. Identify and dispute the Big Bad Thoughts that are creating a mindset of powerlessness, submission, unassertiveness (for example, "I can't handle conflict, I will always be overpowered, and my rights aren't important,") by using the Thought Record Flow Sheet and other debating skills we've emphasized.

Behavioral strategies: Increase assertiveness and improve conflict resolution skills.

Caveat: Assertiveness doesn't guarantee that others will accommodate. In fact, assertiveness can spawn new conflicts, leading to more IDS activation. It is important to choose battles carefully, and to feel sufficiently equipped in assertiveness skills before taking on potentially conflict-filled interpersonal situations. Some people are so lacking in assertiveness skills that they require a behaviorally oriented therapist to help them perfect these skills.

Escape

Sometimes we must simply get away from the sources of extreme stress and defeat. In the case of blocked escape, you must ask yourself if it is really blocked, or if there are beliefs that prevent you from using an available exit. Some situations in which leaving the battle might be appropriate include a job that brings misery and in which any change is unlikely, a demolished marriage with no hope of reconciliation, a toxic friendship/relationship in which strongly opposed personalities clash, or a responsibility beyond your capability (such as job status or full custody of children).

Cognitive strategies: Dispute thoughts that promote guilt and shame about leaving; diminish catastrophic and distorted thoughts blocking escape (for example, "I can't handle change," or "Change is bad, because it will hurt others," or "I have to stick it out at all cost," or "To escape would make me a loser,"); develop problem-solving escape and return-to-power plans.

Behavioral strategies: Apply the anxiety management skills you have learned here, such as relaxation and diaphragmatic breathing; recruit friends, family, etc. to help with change.

Caveat: The thing about escape, however, is that you need to ask yourself if this is related to the causes of your depression. Sometimes, people can feel a great need to escape because they are depressed. This need often focuses on escaping from *the* feelings *of depression itself.* So, some good questions to ask yourself are, "How would I feel about this situation if I were not depressed? Is it possible that when I am not depressed I will see this quite differently?" Now if these questions are difficult to answer, it might be useful to talk the situation over with a good friend or your doctor or therapist to get outside opinions.

There are some situations in which someone might be well aware that their focus on the need to escape from the depression is contributing to the depression, but feel escape is completely impossible. A competent professional therapist can often help a person weigh the costs and benefits of change as well as help him or her determine the most potentially beneficial way of following through.

It is also important to mention that escape as a sole means of dealing with conflict is not advocated. Repeated successful escape can lead to a pattern of avoiding issues. When individuals leave the sources of stress, it is recommended that they find suitable replacements that are reasonably demanding but not overwhelming as soon as possible. Remember, the goal of escape is not just to flee oppression, but to then find another way to feel powerful.

Submit/Subordinate

In "arrested fight" situations, the conflict is prolonged, even though the fight is essentially over. This can occur when individuals believe they have lost unfairly; or simply refuse to accept defeat; or internalize their anger, thereby experiencing injustice or inequity, but not acting on it. Rigid standards and beliefs can be at the root of an arrested fight. For example, some people believe the cost of "giving up" is too high and simply won't accept it. Individuals who challenge established hierarchies often find themselves embroiled in long-term battles. In the workplace, some individuals repeatedly challenge authority, and lose. Accepting a subordinate role is very difficult for some people, as for some, it is tantamount to being "unimportant," "a failure," or "vulnerable."

Cognitive strategies: Call into question beliefs and assumptions that keep you from accepting established hierarchical structures; challenge beliefs as to the value of staying embroiled in a fight that everyone else believes is over; dispute any group pressure that tries to maintain a fighting mode; challenge beliefs and thoughts fueling entitlement and black and white ideas about subordination.

Behavioral strategies: Practice the anger management skills we have discussed here; develop increased assertiveness and conflict resolution skills. Like depression, anger problems are very treatable with cognitive therapy. If you have an anger problem that is interfering with work or relationships, recruiting a skilled clinician would be a good investment.

Accept Defeat and Move On

After a loss has occurred, many people stay acutely entangled in it for months, even years, or they feel unable to move on (e.g., a marital separation in which the shunned spouse is constantly harassing the other). Continuing to remain standing with fists poised after the ref has called the fight just loads defeat upon defeat, and eventually all that anger and resentment will meld into depression.

Cognitive strategies: Using disputation skills, identify and counter shame-based cognitions and distorted assumptions about "loss" and "defeat."

Behavioral strategies: Focus on improving your lifestyle, finding new sources of power, efficacy, worthiness, belonging, etc.

Affiliate/Cooperate

Cooperation reduces conflict, though for some it is not an option, as it is often believed to be tantamount to "knuckling under" or submitting. Such individuals will view problems and conflicts in black and white terms; that is, my way or no way. To cooperate and compromise can result in a conflict resolution in which both parties do not lose their sense of power.

Cognitive strategies: Use the cognitive skills in this book, especially the thought debate strategies, to identify and argue black and white ideas preventing conflict resolution (e.g., "I'm right, you're wrong; there is no in-between").

Behavioral strategies: Develop better assertiveness skills, anger management skills, social skills, and communication skills. Relationships often need an unbiased referee. There are competent marital and relationship counselors out there who can help each partner examine the conflict from different vantage points.

Conflict Free?

Gilbert and his colleagues believe that people with a history of depression may be particularly sensitive to conflict, and have a heightened sense of life as a competition. For example, they may think that if they are not good enough, people will reject them or that they will be valued only if their bodies are thin like a supermodel's. With thoughts like those, they are likely to experience defeat more often. Does this mean that conflicts or competing (trying one's best) should be avoided all the time? No. Conflict is a part of life and cannot always be completely eschewed. Further, relationships often strengthen as a function of conflict resolution; people can grow together by facing up to their differences. The reason we have discussed conflict was to help you recognize and utilize options for avoiding unnecessary conflicts and reducing their duration.

The most import message, though, is whether you fail in a conflict or fail at something you really want out of life, do not turn that failure into a personal defeat that says things about you as person. Be careful not to tell yourself that the defeat makes you inferior or that the defeat means you are not worth anything. Try instead to think of the defeat as a very disappointing setback, and ask yourself what you can learn from it. The more you resist the inner pull of the IDS to see yourself as a low-ranking person without much chance of succeeding in the future, the greater the chances that setbacks in life won't spiral you down into despair.

Main Points

1. A question often asked is why we have depression. Recent research has responded to this question from an evolutionary perspective. The symptoms of depression, researchers believe, served a very valuable purpose in our ancient past in making us back down instead of continuing to fight in defeat situations.

2. Paul Gilbert and his colleagues coined the term Involuntary Defeat Strategy (IDS) to describe the defeat response. In conflicts, there has to be a loser, or both combatants would continue fighting to the death. The IDS occurs when we realize we are losing. It triggers feelings of sadness and shame, thoughts of powerlessness and low self-worth, and a desire to back down. The IDS then serves to end conflicts and help groups accept their rank. The IDS is not the same as depression. Depression occurs when defeats are prolonged, when escape is blocked, when we keep fighting despite the fact that we've lost, or when we ruthlessly shame ourselves for losing.

3. It is important to examine the causes of your depression and determine if you are in a situation of protracted helplessness and defeat, and to recognize what is blocking your return to a stance of self-control and power.

4. Minimizing defeat often requires adopting a new conflict resolution strategy, and people will vary in terms of which strategy will be most likely to remove them from a bog of defeat. For some, fighting harder is the

ticket. Others must remove themselves physically from the source of oppression. Still others must reduce the need to always win, and find a means of compromise and acceptance.

5. Most depressed people must learn to stop beating themselves up for losses and defeats. The idea that losing doesn't make you a loser is a very difficult assumption for many.

Chapter Twelve

Relapse Prevention III: A Lifestyle Upgrade

Our lifestyles should be fertile landscapes, blooming constantly with opportunities to feel a sense of accomplishment, to experience new passions, to laugh, love, and learn. Depression turns your lifestyle into a freezing, treeless, dirt field where every step lands you in a gopher hole and reminds you of nothing but the thousands of other gopher holes riddling the barren badlands for miles in every direction. Coming out of depression is the time to initiate lifestyle change. In fact, there is no better time. If you don't make some changes now in the way you fill your hours as you rise from this horrible patch, when will you?

Significant change in lifestyle becomes progressively more difficult as we age due to real constraints or we may find that we just keep cruising over the same flat landscape, passing opportunity after opportunity, but since "same" isn't killing us, we don't detour and seize more passionate, meaningful opportunities when they arise. This may sound absurd, but if you are coming out of a depression, you have the "benefit" of having a miserable experience in close proximity. Philosophers and poets of old have noted that most people who undergo significant change for the better, as in big, glorious changes they perhaps thought about doing for years but never had the gumption to do, usually do so as they're coming out of a super-bad stretch. It's about seizing the moment. If you miss it, you'll end up back on autopilot cruising through a life of gopher holes.

The Chicken-Egg Issue

What came first—the miserable lifestyle or the depression? Hmmm. Certainly, depression takes its toll on your lifestyle. You cut yourself off from friends and acquaintances and you reduce pleasurable activities and hobbies, and your health often deteriorates. You have to admit, a person who has minimal socialization, eschews new activities, and does nothing but work, eat, and sleep is going to be more vulnerable to depression than one who has a rich, rewarding, multifaceted lifestyle.

Usually it's a combination of both: the depression-caused ashen wasteland of lifestyle, plus some preexisting lifestyle poverty that led to the depression, or at least made it easier for the depressive ogre to come crashing in. Regardless of which came first, I haven't met a depressed person yet who couldn't benefit from a little color enhancement to their waking hours.

But Nothing Seems to Interest Me

It's not uncommon for people who have been depressed for a while to claim that nothing seems appealing in terms of lifestyle changes. Of course nothing "seems" to interest you; you've been depressed for a while, and depression makes lots of things seem different. After weeks or months of living without taking much pleasure in life, we sort of forget what an active, satisfying lifestyle feels like. I've listened to patients express anxiety over leaving the cognitive program. Some will look around and say, "What do I do now?"

Well, let's look at two options: rekindling old hobbies and interests, and taking on some new interests.

Rekindle old hobbies and interests. Go down Memory Lane and list the things you used to do that brought you enjoyment. I mean, year by year. Of course, there will be some things that are no longer enticing, or even appropriate, for you to do now. If listing doesn't float your boat, try journaling. Write a pleasure log, with all the juicy details.

When I'm debating getting back into something I haven't done in a while, a trip to the bookstore will often whet my appetite. I remember thinking once that it would be nice to do some more cooking, and a stroll down the cookbook aisle was just the thing to get me writing grocery lists and driving to different parts of town for hard-to-find ingredients.

The Internet is another incredible resource for finding out how your hobby's been behaving since you dropped it off so long ago. Photo albums can also be helpful to jog your memory. A previously depressed man named Steve once reported to me that he had dug through some old photos and come across some of a trip he and his wife had taken to Maui, during which she had tried jet skiing. Steve didn't get back into jet skiing, but he did get into ocean swimming and snow skiing. Close enough.

Take on new interests. The ascension from depression is a wonderful opportunity to try something new, to take part in things you've never experienced before, and to challenge yourself in ways you might have considered in passing, but never in reality. What have you got to lose? Even if the activity ended up being unsatisfying, it could hardly be as unsatisfying as the past month of depression has been.

So where do you start? Countless folks in the outpatient cognitive therapy program have made school or taking a class a part of their relapse prevention plan. I think our brains get famished if we don't feed them regularly with new knowledge. And I'm not talking about taking advanced calculus, necessarily; rather, just learning something new, calculus or otherwise. Think about all the skills available that you don't have. If you haven't looked through a college or adult education catalog in a while, you will probably be surprised at how many "fun" courses there are along with all the torturous and tedious ones.

What about getting involved in what other people are doing? What's the rage these days? Piggyback square dancing? Sounds like a great way to learn a new skill, meet people, and work on your upper body development. Consider getting involved in an activity a friend or family member enjoys. You might say something like this: "Gee, Gayle. I know I've never expressed interest, but what say I tag along with you guys next time you go bird watching?"

Though the options for filling time are infinite, when you're feeling miserable, it seems like there are only two or three. So, here's a small list that might jog your memory or plant a savory little seed or two.

- A new craft or skill, such as woodworking, needlework, cooking, or quilting.
- Music, whether listening to it, writing it, or playing it.
- A new collection of some object that appeals to you, from duck decoys to stamps or salt shakers.
- A new outside activity, such as gardening, traveling, hiking or fishing.
- A technical skill, such as auto restoration or computer design.
- Volunteer work with a library, a church, or a civic group.
- An activity to improve your physical, mental, or spiritual well being, such as exercise, healthy cooking, meditation, yoga, or a faith-based activity.

After defeating depression, it's important to fill any holes in your lifestyle so new depressions can't sneak in.

Striving for Balance

Dr. Alan Marlatt, a specialist in the realm of addictive behavior, says that ideally, our lives should have a relative balance between sources of stress and methods for reducing stress (1985). Many people with addiction problems, like depressed people, have very impoverished lifestyles, and Marlatt deems it crucial for individuals in recovery to find satisfying replacements to fill the gaping lifestyle holes some feel when they give up alcohol or drugs. He emphasizes a lifestyle schedule that includes exercise, some form of relaxation, positive socialization, and spiritual growth and self-discovery.

I think Marlatt's proposed components of a balanced lifestyle are particularly applicable to depressed people's recovery. Let's review each of these components in turn.

Exercise. This doesn't necessarily mean you need to get out there and start running the 10K tomorrow. Some people think the only exercise worthy of the word is excruciating. Torturous exercise may be the cat's meow for some, but for most folks, there needs to be an element of fun or it will be abandoned.

If solitary exercise seems boring or tedious, try something that involves others. Taking a water aerobics class at the local health club, joining a hiking club, or bike riding with friends are all activities that are more than just exercise. Remember, like many things, more is not necessarily better when it comes to exercise. Don't push your body too far. If you've been idle for a long time, it's always good to get a physical and ask your doctor what the ideal regimen would be.

Relaxation. There are formal relaxation exercises, such as progressive muscle relaxation, and unstructured ones, such as just kicking back. I'm fond of both, but most people will find the unstructured relaxation easier to implement. I consider any activity that enables you to unwind, chill out, kick back or get your mind off of all the demands of life to be a form of relaxation. Reading quietly, driving around, sitting in the hot tub, doodling; those are all ways of relaxing.

Watching TV can be relaxing, but if TV watching is your sole method of relaxation, consider trying some other more creative methods.

Meditation is a form of relaxation. It can be formal, such as yoga, Tai Chi, and other visualization exercises. These can be wonderful lifestyle enhancers, and many people who have recovered from depression whose lives were nothing but stress from wake up to pass out have taken a formal meditation class as part of their relapse prevention plan. You don't need to learn Tai Chi in order to meditate, however. Meditation is any activity that enables you to really disengage. Lying on the lounge and listening to the wind, driving in the rain, and listening to music with headphones could all be considered forms of meditation.

Positive Daily Socialization. This is as opposed to negative socialization, of which we sometimes, unfortunately, have plenty. We need to have contact with the people we get along with in order to orient ourselves. Too much alone time is a drag. Our minds don't like it for the most part, and can start doing funky things. When we're coming out of depression, we don't want to have whole days where we have only the company of our brains. It's too easy then to slip back into self-focused, gloomy thoughts. Some people don't need as much socialization as others, but it is very rare to find someone who is happy being chronically all alone.

Spending time with family is important, but it is also important to nurture relationships outside the family. Some depressed people have let their friendships go by the wayside. If you've done that, now's the time to make that call. Now's the time to evaluate any estrangements or unresolved conflicts with friends. Is it worth it to let them endure? Would it kill you to take the first step toward resolution?

If you don't currently have friends, this is the time to consider changing that. Where do people make friends? Here at home on the couch? No. They make friends at schools, in clubs, through organizations. You have to go where people go. And that's not always enough, either. You have to engage people. You're more likely to make a friend if you put yourself out there and strike up a conversation than if you only enter populated areas when you have to, keep your head down, and talk only when asked a question. As discussed in Chapter Six, if socializing has been a long-standing problem, consider seeing a cognitive-behaviorally oriented therapist to brush up on your social skills or help you diminish social anxiety.

Spirituality and Self-Improvement. I've encountered many depressed people who, as they begin to come out of the murky state, report that they would like to return to their church, or initiate a spiritual course of some kind. Developing and/or enhancing a sense of meaning in life is tremendously important for people who have been bogged down with depression, since what accompanies depression is a feeling that life is nothing but a drudgery or is completely meaningless.

Bad Thoughts Blocking New Activities

The thrust of this book has been intelligent brain over depressive brawn. Below are some cognitive obstacles you might encounter as you use new activities to reach for a healthier lifestyle, and some cognitive disputation comebacks to defeat those obstacles.

I'll look like a fool if I try out something new.

Cognitive Comebacks: Ask yourself, "What would I say to someone I care about if they were worried about this?" Use the Dr. Frankenstein technique (remember, this technique involves building the epitome of your belief, in this example, "a fool," and then comparing yourself to the extreme definition).

I won't be good at it.

Cognitive Comebacks: Decatastrophize "not being good at it." Ask yourself, "So what if I'm not good. Is there punishment for not being the best at something?" Remind yourself that you are trying to make your lifestyle more enjoyable, not perfect. Ask yourself, "Are there things I've tried in the past that I've been able to do well with practice?"

It looks boring, painful, tedious, childish, etc.

Cognitive Comebacks: Ask yourself, "Is this really the concern, or am I just frightened of not being good at it?" Consider evidence from the past that disputes this prediction, or even times in the past when you've thought something was going to be a total drag that ended up being fun or edifying. Remind yourself that you can quit if it turns out to be so terrible, but that you'll never know unless you give it a try.

There are too many other things I need to accomplish.

Cognitive Comebacks: Ask yourself, "Where's the evidence that I won't be able to accomplish things if I add leisure and relaxation to my life?" Do you use your time efficiently, or is there a great deal of time wasted worrying and procrastinating?

I don't deserve to have fun, given all I've neglected while I was depressed.

Cognitive Comebacks: Ask yourself, "What would I say to a dear friend who was worried about this?" Answer as if that friend is coming out a depression and has probably been in a pleasure famine for at least a month or two. Do the Dr. Frankenstein technique (here you would create someone whose deeds render him or her totally undeserving of pleasure, and then compare this monster to yourself).

Passion Making

It's incredible how we meander through life on autopilot with metacognition asleep in the back seat. Have you ever been listening to the radio or watching the television and said, "Hey, this isn't making me happy listening to this commercial," and the turned the channel and found something worthwhile? That's passion making! Now, you might be thinking, "Hmmm. I don't think so," but listen: I can't tell you how often I see people ripping themselves off from precious moments; accepting a table in a restaurant two feet from the malodorous restroom or noisy dish station when there are plenty of more desirable tables; driving the fast route, even though they have sufficient time to drive a quiet beautiful route; sitting through five minutes of awful commercials; or eating a tepid, squished fast food mess while rushing from one task to the next. Very often it seems we have no choices because we aren't really looking around. Increased mindfulness of what we are doing in the moment can help us find options for improving experience; sometimes just a little, other times quite a bit.

Our lives are teeming with fruitful moments to pick. Some moments are cherry sized; some are cantaloupes. It's incredible how people miss so much when it's hanging right there within reach. Consider this scenario: Jeff is standing in the kitchen reading the paper before work. The kids are watching TV and hustling to get ready for school. Jeff looks outside and notices that the sunrise is amazing. There is a chair outside, aimed right at that great view. Jeff looks at his watch, and realizes that he has about 10 minutes to spare before he has to leave. There is effort in folding the paper, picking up the coffee cup, leaving the house, perhaps wiping the dust off the chair, but he does so any way. Jeff seizes the moment and spends 10 minutes watching the sky turn from pink to orange to fluffy white and indigo. He smells the honeysuckle behind him. He listens to a morning bird. Jeff has taken the reins of time and consciousness.

Imagine being so conscious that you make Jeff-like decisions 20 times an hour. Uncomfortable chair in the waiting room? Change chairs. Sun's in your eyes? Get up and close the blinds. View boring? Move. Sunset beautiful? Get closer to it; drive the scenic route. Stomach craving fruit bat shish kabob tonight? Well, drive across town to the fruit bat shish kabob stand and get some. I call this hyperawareness of here-and-now control passion making.

Passion making takes extra work. You have to lean forward and move the vase slightly so you can witness the perfectly blooming rose. You have to leave the car there in the garage and walk back upstairs to get that audiotape you forgot, the one that would make the morning's dreary bumper-to-bumper drive a little bit better.

Passion making as a mission is more than making your day a little better. It's powerful depression self-treatment too. Think about it; it is the act of improving something a little with the result that you reduce discomfort, enhance mood, beautify the view, or stretch a good time. Each and every time you do this, it is stored as a memory, a memory of reinforcement. (Diminishing something negative is called *negative reinforcement*; increasing something positive is called *positive reinforcement*.) Depression is about powerlessness. Passion making kicks the dismal state of depression with a happier experience; one in which you've taken control, bequeathed yourself something nice, and made your future a little better by tinkering with what's lying there in reach.

Main Points

1. Lifestyle enhancement may be the most important aspect of relapse prevention. Coming out of depression is an ideal time to initiate lifestyle change; in fact, historically, the coming out of a bad period is when people are most likely to make change for the better. The motivation is to not return to where you've just been. Some people had perfectly balanced and enjoyable lifestyles before they were depressed. For them, re-igniting previous passions is the order. For individuals who had impoverished lifestyles to begin with, the challenge is more difficult. It may involve taking on activities that were a part of life some years ago, or trying things entirely new.

2. Exercise, relaxation, positive socialization, and meditation or spiritual development are believed to be vital to
a balanced happy lifestyle. Exercise does not have to be
a masochistic endeavor; in fact, the more fun the regimen, the more likely it is you'll stick with it. There are
formal relaxation techniques, such as progressive muscle relaxation and massage, but any activity that
enables you to kick back and unwind is just as legitimate. When it comes to depression, social support has
a strong connection to well being. Regular contact with
positive people also keeps us from sinking back into
worry and negative self-focus. A form of relaxation,
meditation can be structured, such as yoga or imagery,
or unstructured, such as lying under a tree and interpreting cloud formations.

3. Cognitive obstacles often get in the way when we try to
engage in something new. Such beliefs as "I won't be
good at it," and "I don't deserve to have fun," can be
challenged by using the thought debate tools presented
in previous chapters.

4. *Passion making* involves increasing consciousness of
your power to improve the here and now. Asking yourself, "What could I do to improve this moment a little?"
puts you in a position to reward yourself. Frequent passion making strengthens beliefs of worthiness and self-
control, which are good buffers against depression.

Chapter Thirteen:

Concluding Remarks and a Few Words about Therapy

When Richard said, just in conversation, that his experience with depression felt like having an ogre on his chest, I doubt he had any idea that his mythical character would end up being the primary metaphor, or mascot, for a self-help book about depression. Ogres are fictitious creatures, but there's nothing fictitious about depression, although many people who have not experienced depression have no idea how the condition can impair a person. I hope that this book has provided you with a thorough understanding of depression and how it endures, and has given you some powerful new tools for getting rid of the awful condition and making its return less likely.

My motivation to write this book stemmed from my observation that information alone is often enough to encourage people to make changes, even lasting changes. I've listened to patients, as well as friends, report that something they read was the primary impetus for making changes, and I know it from my own life as well. Many people simply need to know what to do. Often, people don't make any changes for the better simply because the missing puzzle piece has not been discovered. Once that missing piece is fitted, they're off and running.

I've loaded each chapter with advice on how to get out of an episode of depression and prevent its reoccurrence. Cognitive therapy is fairly well known, and I'll sometimes hear people discussing it in an overly simplistic way. My hope is that this presentation of cognitive therapy's details will give you the missing puzzle piece.

Does this mean that this book is necessarily all you need to break depression or to keep you from falling back into that wretched quagmire at a later time? Maybe. Maybe not. Change is very difficult, especially when what you want to change has established itself as immobile and has blocked any foreseeable pathway.

When people have been unable to rid themselves of depression on their own, I always advocate that they get some professional help, and the sooner the better. The rule with depression is that the longer the episode lasts, the harder it is to break. If you're still depressed after reading this book, it doesn't mean that you are unintelligent, unmotivated, or a hopeless case. It means your depression is a strong one, and that it needs more than just a self-help tool.

Depression can be so tenacious that self-help resources can't even scrape it. In fact, if your depression has seriously influenced important areas of your life, like work, health, or relationships, and if you are having even vague suicidal thoughts, you should seek an evaluation by a qualified clinician. A psychiatrist is ideal, but your family doctor is a good place to start, so any medical causes of the depression can be ruled out and the doctor can direct you to an appropriate specialist if needed. It's been said throughout the book, but if you are experiencing depression, do consider talking with your doctor about antidepressant medication. It doesn't make you "weak" if you are getting help from a medication. Nor is taking an antidepressant medication in any way akin to taking street drugs. Some people mistakenly believe antidepressant medication is tantamount to taking an addictive substance, but it isn't. It's like someone with an injury taking an anti-inflammatory. It's about taking advantage of medical resources that may help you get out of a painful condition.

Individual or group cognitive behavior therapy is also worth considering. I'm a big fan of cognitive behavior therapy, obviously, and though this book covers a great deal, it could never mirror what a real live therapy experience with a competent clinician can achieve.

Cognitive behavior therapy is one of many kinds of therapy, and if the philosophy of this book seems reasonable, you might consider starting therapy with a cognitive behavioral therapist. Most cities have a local psychological association or referral center that can give you the names of their members who focus on cognitive behavioral strategies.

I have a great deal of faith in group therapy; in fact, it's my preferred method of treating depression. Many depressed people come to therapy because of interpersonal difficulties. A cognitively oriented group not only teaches people to use cognitive coping tools, but also offers opportunities to actually use them with other human beings (other than the therapist), some of whom may actually push your buttons, thus giving you an opportunity to deal with conflict differently.

We've discussed that the internalized or arrested anger is often a significant contributor to depression. People with internalized anger often do very well in group therapy. Frequently, a person who internalizes anger will talk about how she has been mistreated, but express no anger whatsoever about it. Others in the group will express anger, however. Then, the therapy session becomes an opportunity for the person who internalizes anger to witness what a normal response would be to her situation, and an encouragement for her to apply some of the feedback offered by others in way that can help her actually experience an appropriate, tolerable level of anger. The safe, structured group forum then becomes a place for experimenting with anger, letting it rise to an appropriate level, using problem-solving techniques to find various resolutions, and practicing assertive strategies.

Appendix

On Suicidal Thoughts

Not everyone who is depressed experiences suicidal thoughts. Some do, however, and it is certainly the most serious of all depressive symptoms. The successful suicide of a person is a horrible tragedy; horrible for the victim's family and horrible in terms of a lost life that may have found meaning, purpose and happiness if the depression had been effectively treated.

Below are my strong recommendations if you are having even mild, passive suicidal thoughts:

1. *Don't keep them to yourself.* Tell someone who will listen. And tell them specifically what you are thinking. There is a big difference between having vague thoughts of death and having active urges to do yourself in immediately. If the person you talk to doesn't take you seriously and responds with something like, "Oh, Jerry, you're fine. Buck up. Gotta go," then you need to tell someone else, someone who will take you seriously.

2. *Don't worry about burdening a loved one.* Even if the person you call is cranky about being awakened at 2 A.M., the cost of getting up is significantly less to that person in the long run than the cost if you were to follow through with the thoughts.

3. *If your urge to act on the idea of suicide is strong, that is, you have a plan and you are having medium to strong urges to act on it, call an emergency hotline.* If you can't find the right number, call 9-1-1 or go to an emergency room. Some people fear hospitalization, and don't tell others because they fear they'll be locked up. Times have changed. It is rare for depressed people to be involuntarily hospitalized for long periods of time. However, a locked unit is the best place for an actively suicidal person. Some people, if hospitalized briefly, get a chance to talk to trained staff, work out a recovery plan with their

doctor, have their medication evaluated, and get a brief respite from their life stressors. I've seen patients who report that their suicidal thoughts have gone away after just 24 hours on a locked psychiatric unit. Further, calling a hotline will not necessarily land you in the hospital. A compassionate, trained counselor available to talk to you for a while sometimes can help you unplug the suicidal thoughts to the extent that a less intensive level of treatment is appropriate, like outpatient therapy, or an appointment with a psychiatrist for medication consideration.

4. *Utilize the mental health system.* Most cities have a local psychological association or mental health referral services, staffed with people who know what is available in your community. And when it comes to therapists, if you have a negative experience, don't abandon the whole field. Bad matches happen. But there are also extremely competent, compassionate clinicians who can help you. If you feel the therapist is inadequately trained, non-empathic, or just a bad match, talk with him or her about your impressions. If that doesn't help, fire that therapist and find someone else, or consider using another referral source.

5. *See a medical doctor to talk about an antidepressant medication.* I have a lot of faith in antidepressant medication, and, in collaborating with physicians in the treatment of depressed people, have found that medications plus therapy are usually the best regimen. Some people can get out of depression without medications, but try to have an open mind. If you've been trying to get out of a depression for over a month and think taking medication is some sort of weakness, consider taking yourself and your pride down to the doctor's office and giving medication a try. Remember, no one can force you to take a pill. If you don't like it, spit it out. But for Pete's sake, consider taking advantage of the recent developments in medications that treat depression and

similar illnesses. There are drugs that can really give depression the fist blow it deserves. Depression is no different than other medical problems in terms of how debilitating it can be. Regardless of its cause, depression has targetable biological elements. For a very depressed person to deprive himself of a well-targeted medicine would be like a person with severe arthritis depriving himself from a good anti-inflammatory agent.

6. *Don't fool yourself with thoughts like "This will pass," if you are having suicidal thoughts.* Untreated depressions can worsen. The earlier you get help, the easier it is to blast the depression. Depression's ugly butt can be kicked. This book may give you some good uppercuts and knee-to-groin lunges. But if you are having suicidal thoughts, you definitely need more. Go and get it.

References

Abramson, L.Y., Seligman, E.P., & Teasdale, J.D. (1978). Learned helplessness in humans: critique and reformulation. *Journal of Abnormal Psychology, 87 (1)*, 49-74.

Beck, A.T. (1963). Thinking in depression: 1, Idiosyncratic content and cognitive distortions. *Archives of General Psychiatry, 9*, 324-333.

Beck, A.T., Shaw, B.F., Rush, J.A., & Emery, G. (1979). *Cognitive therapy of depression*. New York: Guilford Publications.

Bellack, A.S., Hersen, M., & Himmelhoch, J.M. (1983). A comparison of social skills training, pharmacotherapy and psychotherapy for depression. *Behaviour Research and Therapy, 21*, 101-107.

Blackburn, I.M., & Moore, R.G. (1997). Controlled acute and follow-up trial of cognitive therapy in out-patients with recurrent depression. *British Journal of Psychiatry, 171*, 328-334.

Bower, G.H. (1981). Mood and memory. *American Psychologist, 36*, 129-148.

Burgess, I. S., Jones, L. N., Robertson, S.A., Radcliffe, W.N., Emerson, E., Lawler, P., & Crow, T. J. (1981). The degree of control exerted by phobic and non-phobic verbal stimuli over the recognition behaviour of phobic and non-phobic subjects. *Behaviour Research and Therapy, 19*, 223-234.

Burns, D.D. (1980) *Feeling good: The new mood therapy*. New York: William Morrow.

Butler, G., & Mathews, A. (1987). Anticipatory anxiety and risk perception. *Cognitive Therapy and Research, 11*, 551-565.

Clark, D.M., & Teasdale, J.D. (1982). Diurnal variation in clinical depression and accessibility of memories of positive and negative experiences. *Journal of Abnormal Psychology, 91*, 97-95.

Clark, D.A., & Teasdale, J.D. (1985). Constraints on the effects of mood on memory. *Journal of Personality and Social Psychology, 48*, 1595-1608.

Clark, L. A. (1989). The anxiety and depressive disorders: Descriptive psychopathology and differential diagnosis. In P. C. Kendall & D. Watson (Eds.), *Anxiety and depression: Distinctive and overlapping features* (pp. 83-129). San Diego: Academic Press.

Cohen, S. & Willis, T.A. (1985). Stress, social support, and the buffering hypothesis. *Psychological Bulletin, 98*, 310-357.

Cohen, D.J., Eckhardt, C.I., & Schagat, K. D. (1998). Attention allocation and habituation to anger-related stimuli during a visual search task. *Aggressive Behavior. 24 (6)*, 399-409.

DiGuiseppe, R. (1999). Assessment, Diagnosis and Treatment of Clients with Anger Problems. Workshop sponsored by Lima Associates: Carlsbad.

Eckhardt, C. I., & Cohen, D. J. (1997). Attention to anger-relevant and irrelevant stimuli following naturalistic insult. *Personality & Individual Differences,* 23 (4), 619-629.

Feindler, E. L. (1990). Adolescent Anger Control. Half-day workshop sponsored by the Association for the Advancement of Behavior Therapy, November 3, 1990. San
Francisco, California.

Feindler, E.L. (1991). Cognitive strategies in anger control interventions for children and adolescents. In P.C. Kendall (Ed.), Child and adolescent therapy. *Cognitive behavioral procedures.* New York: Guilford Publications.

Feindler, E.L. & Ecton, R.B. (1988). *Adolescent anger control: Cognitive behavioral techniques.* New York: Pergamon.

Garber, J. & Flynn, C. (2001). Vulnerability to depression in childhood and adolescence. In R.E. Ingram, & J. M. Price (Eds.), *Vulnerability to psychopathology: Risk across the lifespan.* New York: Guilford.

Gilbert, P. (1992). *Depression: The evolution of powerlessness.* New York: Guilford.

Gilbert, P. (1997). *Overcoming depression: A step-by-step approach to gaining control over depression.* UK: Oxford.

Gilbert, P. (2000). Varieties of submissive behavior as forms of social defense: Their evolution and role in depression. In L. Sloman, & P. Gilbert (Eds.), *Subordination and defeat: An evolutionary approach to mood disorders and their therapy.* London: Erlbaum.

Gotlib, I. H., & Cane, D. B. (1989). Self-report assessment of depression and anxiety.
In P. C. Kendall, & D. Watson (Eds.), *Anxiety and depression: Distinctive and overlapping features* (pp. 131-169). San Diego, CA: Academic Press.

Hollon, S.D., DeRubeis, R.J., Evans, M.D., Wiemer, M.J., Garvey, M.J., Grove, W.M., & Tuason, V.B. (1992). Cognitive therapy and pharmacotherapy for depression: Singly and in combination. *Archives of General Psychiatry,* 49, 774-781.

Ingram, R.E. (1984). Toward an information processing analysis of depression.*Cognitive Therapy and Research,* 8, 443-478.

Ingram, R.E., & Kendall, P.C. (1986). Cognitive clinical psychology: Implications of an information processing perspective. In R.E. Ingram (Ed.), *Information processing approaches to clinical psychology* (pp. 3-21). Orlando, FL: Academic Press.

Kendall, P.C. (1990). Healthy thinking. *Behavior Therapy.* 23, 1-11.

Lazarus, R.S. (1966). Psychological stress and the coping process. New York: McGraw-Hill.

Lazarus, R.S. & Folkman, S. (1984). *Stress appraisal and coping.* New York: Springer.

Lazarus, R.S. & Launier, R. (1978). Stress-related transactions between person and environment. In L.A. Pervin, & M. Lewis (Eds.), *Perspectives in interactional psychology*. New York: Plenum.

Lepore, S. J. (1992). Social conflict, social support, and psychological distress: Evidence of cross-domain buffering effects. *Journal of Personality and Social Psychology, 63*, 857-867.

Little, V.L., & Kendall, P.C. (1979). Cognitive-behavioral interventions with delinquents: Problem-solving, role-taking and self-control. In P.C. Kendall, & S.D. Hollon (Eds.), *Cognitive behavioral interventions: Theory, research and practice*. New York: Academic Press.

Lochman, J. (1984). Psychological characteristics and assessment of aggressive adolescents. In C. R. Keith (Ed.), *The aggressive adolescent: Clinical perspectives*. New York: The Free Press.

MacLoed, C., & Mathews, A.M. (1991). Cognitive-experimental approaches to the emotional disorders. In P.R. Martin (Ed.), *Handbook of behavior therapy and psychological science: An integrative approach*. New York: Pergamon.

Marlatt, G. A. (1978). Craving for alcohol, loss of control, and relapse: A cognitive-behavioral analysis. In P.E. Nathan, G.A. Marlatt, & T. Løberg (Eds.), Alcoholism: *New directions in behavioral research and treatment*. New York: Plenum.

Marlatt, G.A. (1985). Lifestyle Modification. In G.A. Marlatt, & J.R. Gordon (Eds.), *Relapse prevention*. New York: Guilford Publications.

Marsland, D.W., Wood, M., & Mayo, F. (1976). Content of family practice: A data bank for patient care, curriculum, and research in family practice-526,196 patient problems. *Journal of Family Practice, 3*, 25-68.

Miller, W.R., & Rollnick, S. (1991). *Motivational interviewing: Preparing people to change addictive behavior*. New York: Guilford Publications.

Novaco, R.W. (1979). The cognitive regulation of anger and stress. In P. Kendall, & S. Hollon (Eds.), *Cognitive-behavioral interventions: Theory, research and procedures*. New York: Academic Press.

Parkinson, L., & Rachman, S. (1981). Speed of recovery from an uncontrived stress. *Advances in Behaviour Research and Therapy, 3*, 119-123.

Price, J.S. (1972). Genetic and phylogenetic aspects of mood variations. *International Journal of Mental Health, 1*, 124-144.

Prochaska, J.O. & DiClemente, C.C. (1982) Transtheoretical therapy: Toward a more integrative model of change. *Psychotherapy: Theory, Research and Practice, 19*, 276-288.

Prochaska, J.O., Norcross, J.C., DiClemente, C.C. (1994). *Changing for good: The revolutionary program that explains the six stages of change and teaches you how to free yourself from bad habits*. New York: William Morrow.

Rhodes, W. S., Riskind, J. H., & Lane, J. W. (1987). Emotional states and memory biases: Effects of cognitive priming and mood. *Journal of Personality and Social Psychology, 52*, 91-99.

Seligman, M.E.P., Abramson, L., Semmel, A., & von Baeyer, C. (1979). Depressive attributional style. *Journal of Abnormal Psychology, 88*, 242-248.

Smith, T.W., & Greenberg, J. (1981). Depression and self focused attention. *Motivation and Emotion, 5*, 323-331.

Wolpe, J. (1958). *Psychotherapy by reciprocal inhibition*. Stanford, CA: Stanford University Press.